Eating the Elephant
One Bite at a Time

—52 Weekly Lessons In Leadership

Brian Klemmer

VIP
VISION IMPRINTS PUBLISHING
A Thomas Nelson Company

www.thomasnelson.com

Tulsa, Oklahoma

EATING THE ELEPHANT ONE BITE AT A TIME
© 2006 by Brian Klemmer

Vision Imprints Publishing
8801 S. Yale, Suite 410
Tulsa, OK 74137
918-493-1718

ISBN 1-599510-26-X
Library of Congress catalog card number: 2006926162

Printed in the United States of America

Contents

Acknowledgments

This book is dedicated to Tom Willhite who was the most significant adult mentor I had in teaching me about life success. He led me to Christ, he taught me the fundamental principles our Klemmer and Associate Leadership seminars are built on, he opened up a whole new world of possibilities to me. I knew him for nine years and worked for him for 7 before he was killed in 1983. Many of my lessons came about simply watching him live life and run a company. Sometimes he specifically would take me somewhere or have me do things specifically to teach me something. Some of the stories in this book are actually events I experienced with him. If this book in some way impacts your life so that you experience some of the fulfillment and success I have had, then the book will be worth it.

His life was not perfect. He had some serious flaws as many people do. Yet he affected my life in a way I will always be grateful. That is a great lesson in itself. If you had to wait for someone to be perfect to learn from we wouldn't be learning. You can learn from anyone if you have the right mindset. I will owe him for the rest of my life and I want to honor him with this book.

I also want to acknowledge my parents Ken & Alice Klemmer who raised me with love, a sense of duty to mankind, a willingness to work hard, and a desire to do the right thing as best I know at the time.

Thanks to Brian Mast who has edited this book as well as my first two books in a valiant effort to make a writer out of a speaker. Thanks to John Mason and his crew for all the work that goes into publishing and believing in me as a writer.

Thanks last but not least to my loving wife Roma and children Kelly, David, and Krystal in whom I am all very proud.

Introduction

In creating sustained change there is a three-step process we call ARC: Awareness, Responsible action, Correction. Once a person has an insight or awareness it needs to be translated into some kind of action. Without action you have information not transformation. Even after change occurs there are conditions in an organization or person's life that push the person or organization into going in an old direction. These conditions are similar to tides, currents, or wind pushing a boat into an old direction after a rudder change. This book is broken into 52 lessons with the desire that with one lesson read and applied every week there will be a constant pressure applied like a rudder to keep you going and growing in positive leadership for a one-year period. Each lesson has a principle to increase your insight on leadership, a story illustrating the principle, very specific take a way lessons, and specific action steps to integrate into your life that week. As you do this you will gain increased awareness around the principle and start the process all over again. If you are disciplined enough to take this approach you will acquire a depth to your leadership even only a few aspire to.

You may also use these lessons within a department our team. As you collectively discuss, apply, and question the principles and action steps you will be in effect digesting the ideas and making them a part of your organization. This amplifies or leverages the information because of the accountability this creates in its application.

Email us your success stories at mastery@klemmer.com so we can include them in future editions. May you enjoy the journey and the impact you will have on others. Making a difference together.

—Brian Klemmer
President, Klemmer & Associates Leadership Seminars Inc.

Carrots, Eggs, and Coffee

—Leaders change the situation instead of being changed by the situation

What are you most like: a carrot, an egg, or coffee?

A **carrot** starts out firm, but when you put a carrot in boiling water it becomes limp. An **egg** starts out with a hard shell and is soft in the middle, but place it in boiling water and the inside becomes hard. And when you put **coffee** in boiling water, it changes the water completely.

What challenges have you been experiencing in your career, family life, physically or spiritually? Think of any of those situations as the boiling water.

Some people are like carrots. Oh, they act tough enough, but the challenges of life soften them, they wilt and won't stand up for themselves any more.

Other people are like eggs. As they confront challenges they get hard on the inside. They're calloused, they become unable or unwilling to feel and do not allow themselves to connect and relate with other people.

Leaders are like coffee. When thrust into the challenges of life they actually change the situation.

Have you been a carrot, egg, or coffee? Buy some coffee, even if you don't normally drink it, and put it in a bowl on your desk. Let that "trigger" you to be a leader who, like coffee, changes the situation you are in for the better.

As a child, I saw people as one of two types: There were the nice caring compassionate people. They didn't seem to make much happen, didn't date the nicest girls or guys, and weren't movers and shakers. Then there were the people that made things happen, but they were often arrogant, hard, and self-centered.

It didn't seem fair. I wanted to be compassionate and caring and yet able to change the world. I wanted to be what I now call a "Compassionate Samurai:" a warrior with a heart for service and contribution.

That's what it will take to change things, like the fact that one out of every eight children drops out of school in the USA, rampant illiteracy in the world, a marriage that is not working, or a satisfying career in an uncertain economy.

Carrots and eggs won't do it. This week, be like coffee. Be a Compassionate Samurai, a warrior with a heart for service and contribution who alters the world you live in.

TAKEAWAY!

Leaders change the situation, so even after they leave, things are different than when they arrived.

Action Step #1

Buy a bag of coffee and put it on your desk as a trigger device.

Action Step #2

Write a brief paragraph describing the biggest challenge you face in your life right now. Then, write another short paragraph on exactly how you'd like your life to be in that area right now. And finally, write a sentence that describes one specific action you will take this week—no matter how big or small it seems to you—to change your life to being exactly how you'd like it to be.

An Example

Early in my career in the seminar business, my mentor sent me to San Diego to save the failing market there. The seminars were so poorly attended they were considering closing down our San Diego office.

When I arrived, I noticed that a lot of teenagers were hanging around the office. The environment and feeling created by all those kids was driving away the more conservative, successful business people we also wanted to bring into our seminars. Like attracts like.

The teenagers were good people who deserved to be supported and served, but it was hurting our bigger market. So I created another place for the kids to hangout and made it clear they were not to be around our office.

It was not an especially popular action for many of our seminar graduates, but it changed how the rest of us thought about the organization and who we attracted. Within a short period of time, San Diego was a thriving market for our seminars.

That is what coffee is all about!

"What we are depends mainly on what we look for"
—John Lubbock

The Desire for Air
—Leaders create needs vs. waiting to be imposed on by a need

Plato's mentor was Socrates. Plato thought Socrates was the wisest person of this time and he passionately desired to learn all of Socrates' wisdom.

Legend has it that one day Socrates and Plato were walking down the beach deep in conversation. At one point, Socrates said to Plato, "Walk with me into the ocean." They turned and walked into the sea together.

Now, in your imagination, picture that happening: Student and teacher, two of the greatest philosophers of history, striding into the surf side by side.

The water started out around their ankles, then rose up to their knees. As the water got higher Plato wondered, "What is the lesson my master is trying to teach me?"

When the water was about shoulder height, Socrates abruptly grabbed Plato's head and pushed him down under the water. As Plato was held down, he undoubtedly wondered again what this lesson was all about.

After a time, when Plato ran out of air, he began to struggle to get his head above water. He punched and kicked and grabbed to get free, but Socrates was a strong man and held him down. Finally, Plato blacked out due to lack of oxygen. Socrates pulled him ashore and resuscitated him.

When Plato regained consciousness, he angrily accused Socrates of trying to drown him. Socrates matter-of-factly explained, "If that had been my intention, I would not have pulled you ashore."

"Then why did you do that?" Plato demanded.

Socrates calmly replied, "When you desire my knowledge like you desired that breath of air, then you shall have it."

So many people desire things, but they want them only at an intellectual level. They wish for a wildly romantic long lasting relationship, for financial independence, for fame, or to make a difference in other people's lives, but for most people, they do not desire it like Plato wanted that breath of air.

Leaders allow, and even encourage, themselves to desire. They create a hunger for things that is as strong as Plato's desire for air.

Only with a large hunger will you put up with the large discomfort and inconvenience required to be successful. This is the single biggest reason why people aren't more successful in life and work. They don't truly NEED it.

The answer is to first create the NEED, then you shall have it.

This is a practical reason for thinking bigger. It is too easy to provide for yourself and even your family. You must go on a hunt to find something more or better that moves you.

Open up to how awful it feels to not be able to read and how you can do something about it, and you will be compelled to take action. Go to a third world country and actually watch someone die of starvation and know that your commitment and cash could have stopped that child from dying.

What spark of desire will you ignite this week? How will you fan those flames into a bonfire of desire?

TAKEAWAY!

Develop a hunger for something important. Challenge and test the people you are mentoring or who are your next layer of management or leadership.

Action Step #1

Pick something that truly matters to you that you desire. Visit it. Literally, spend time with that desire and recall all the specific reasons you want that. Share your desire and reasons with select family members and friends.

An Example

> Let's say you want a new home. Write down the tangible reasons (i.e. investment value, shorter commute, etc.), pleasure reasons (i.e. recreation, relaxation, etc.), and emotional reasons (i.e. how it will make you feel in terms of freedom, security, self-esteem, etc.).

Action Step #2

Pick prospective leaders from among your key business partners or teammates and give them a test. Individually, have them tackle an ongoing problem. Perhaps it is a negative person or a situation that isn't being resolved. Give them something meaningful to do, but put them in over their head, too. This is how they get stronger and build muscles. You can be their lifeline if they start to drown.

An Example

> The major mentor in my life for eight years was a man named Tom Willhite. He died in a plane accident at the age of 43.

Tom's dream was to build a college, but he didn't live long enough to see that. To pay him back for all I learned from him, I committed to raising $4 million dollars and putting up an educational facility.

To build my desire into a bonfire of passion, I started by looking at the original plans Tom had and later at the actual architectural drawings. In the middle of the fund-raising campaign, I brought many of the key donors to the actual land and we walked around as the building was going up. I visualized memories of conversations Tom and I had about his dream and I pretended I was showing him the completed buildings in my mind. I imagined his satisfaction and my pride.

This fanning of the flames of desire is crucial, especially when you hit tough spots where things aren't working as planned or going as well as you want. It helps you refocus and recommit and gives you renewed energy to complete your project.

"The more thou dost advance, the more thy feet pitfalls will meet. The Path that leadeth on is lighted by one fire- the light of daring burning in the heart. The more one dares, the more he shall obtain. The more he fears, the more that light shall pale—and that alone can guide."
—Aristotle

Giving to Get

—Leaders work on giving more than they work on getting

The famous statesman and prime minister of England, Sir Winston Churchill, once said, "We make a living by what we get. We make a life by what we give."

Do you spend more time on what you are getting out of your job, such as your salary, or on how much you can give to the receptionist, to your boss, to someone in another department, going that extra mile for your customer?

Do you spend more time on what you are getting out of a personal relationship or on what you can give to it?

How can you give more this week? Take a moment now to think of all you can give to people.

If you are in networking, you have a product, service, and a business opportunity to give people. If you are a partner, manager, or employee, you can give to people on your team by giving them encouragement, assistance, and support.

You can give to people who are stumbling or stuck by giving them a nudge to take action when they are scared or complacent. You can give to people by really listening to them. You can give to people by stretching them in what they believe they can be, and do and have. You can give someone money or time or knowledge.

Remember that giving or being of service is giving to others what they truly need and want, and not simply what you want to give them.

You can also give to yourself. Sometimes—many times—we overlook that in our giving to others. Maybe you give time to family, church, community, but don't take any time for yourself. Perhaps taking an hour walk just for you would be a great gift to give yourself.

Can you give more this week to others and yourself than you did last week? Keep track of your giving this week with a simple list or a "Giving Journal." Remember, you make a living by what you GET and you make a life by what you GIVE.

TAKEAWAY!

Remember to make a life, not just a living. Ask the people you meet how it is that you can support or give to them, instead of assuming what it is they want. Give time, money, respect to yourself as much as you give to others.

Action Step #1

Take one day this week and focus on giving to people who you do not expect to receive anything from in return.

An Example

If you are in the field operations of your company, call the corporate accounting department and ask how you can support them or send a gift (like a pizza for lunch) to the people in customer service. Write a "thank you" note and include it in a bill you are paying. Put a dollar bill in an envelope and send it to a stranger. Pay the toll for the car behind you.

Notice how this giving with "no strings attached" makes you feel.

Action Step #2

Take a significant part of one day this week and give it to yourself. Any needs or demands from family, business, and the community should go on a different day. Write down how you felt about what you did and how you felt at the end of the day.

An Example

Pick something you enjoy that you haven't done in a while, such as reading for pleasure, going for a walk in a park, watching a movie, having coffee with friends, or simply spending quiet time by yourself.

> "If love is the answer could someone repeat the question"
> —Lily Tomlin

Context Changes Content

—Leaders set the context for their organization

Write the following word down and brand it on your mind: CONTEXT

I am going to suggest that context can make or break you and your organization (by which I mean any group of people working, playing, or living together).

Have you ever heard someone say, "You took that out of context?" Context is the surrounding or environment you're in. When you take something out of context, you have changed the environment and that changes the *content*.

If I have a glass jar with jellybeans in it, the glass jar is the context and the jellybeans are the content. If I change the context from a glass jar to a smelly old trash can, then I have changed the content from candy to garbage.

One of the jobs of leaders is to set the context for their organization (and themselves). What context are you setting for your organization, group, team, and partnerships?

Is your context one of risk taking, behaving as the victim in certain circumstances, acceptance, excitement, or honesty? What context are you setting in your family life? You set context not by telling people about it, but by BEING.

You are the context for your organization; they are the content. You often change results not by trying to change the result, but by changing the context. If you want your business or family results to be different, then maybe you need to change the context of your organization by changing how you are being.

How will being bold, vulnerable, compassionate, honest, or accountable affect your organization or family, thereby producing the results you want? Look and see.

TAKEAWAY!
Context changes content. It is the leaders' job to set the context for their organization.

Action Step #1

Each day this week, choose a value, quality, or aspect of character and focus on making that your context for the day. Keep a journal and write down each day's context and report what happened. End your journal each day by answering the question: "What's the best thing that happened to me today?"

An Example

Start the first day with a quality that is one of your strengths, such as organization, giving, creativity, patience, or enthusiasm. Toward the end of your week, pick a value you are not so strong with and try it on for size as your context. For example: If you are a pretty serious person, have the context for the day be playfulness or fun.

Action Step #2

Create a context of More and Better.

An Example

On your next trip, rent a hotel room one level more expensive than you normally would and rent a car one level more expensive. If you're not traveling this week, have lunch at a "higher class" restaurant, purchase a more costly item than you normally would, or give a more expensive gift to someone. Set a context that you are worth a lot.

One of my very good friends is Bob Harrison, a Christian minister who speaks to large audiences around the world. He supports people in increasing the quality of their life in every way, relationships, financially, spiritually, and physically. He holds a seminar for leaders once a year. To set the context of increase, it is always in Hawaii at a luxury hotel.

> "It is no use walking anywhere to preach unless our walking is our preaching."
> —St. Francis of Assisi

Change Your Viewpoint

—Leaders change their viewpoints and assist others in doing so to reveal their blind spots

Ophthalmologists are eye doctors. They have a name for a blind spot on the eye: it's called a scotoma. If you have a scotoma, you can see all around something, but not where the blind spot is. So, if I am looking right at you, I might be able to see your whole face, except for your nose.

Now, I can either cure the blind spot or I can change my viewpoint. If I take two steps to the left, then I still have my scotoma or blind spot, but now, with this new viewpoint, I can see your whole face and your nose, too.

Many times we want a result badly, but we do not see achieving it as realistic. That's simply a blind spot we have.

You can shift a blind spot through brainstorming with other people where you are offered someone else's viewpoint. Blind spots can be healed by having a revelation, even an emotional experience that alters their viewpoint of reality.

The author who wrote the famous song, "Amazing Grace," had such a revelation. He was a 26-year-old slave trader on his way from Africa to the United States in the early 1800's. His ship ran into a deadly storm. He prayed to God for a miracle. The storm cleared and he and the ship were saved. He returned immediately to Africa and released all 120 slaves. He then went to England and became a leader of the abolitionist movement.

Many times the life experiences required to have a revelation are too expensive. That's why experiential learning in a good seminar or with a great coach can be so valuable. You can have the benefit of healing a scotoma and not pay anywhere near the cost that life often requires.

The Greek word "metanoia" means to change your viewpoint. The word "sin," in old English, was yelled by someone standing near an archery target to indicate you missed the bull's eye in the center. Feeling guilty is not the focus. If you missed the mark, change your viewpoint and you will hit the mark.

What can you do this week to change a viewpoint that is not giving and getting you the results you want?

TAKEAWAY!

If you're not achieving the results you want, you probably have blind spots that are obscuring your viewpoint. A deeply emotional experience can alter your viewpoint in an instant.

Action Step #1

Look at your personal or professional life and pick out a goal you are struggling to accomplish or any situation that isn't the way you want it to be.

Now, meet with two or three people from different professions than yours or who have vastly different interests or experiences. Brainstorm with them, asking what they would do if they were you? No reasons for why it can't be done are allowed. Your job is to listen. Let each person contribute ways to improve your result. It doesn't mean you have to do exactly what they say. Your goal is to change your viewpoint, so you don't sin and miss the target.

An Example

In 1981, I hired a lady from Idaho to come to San Diego to build our seminar business. Two days after she arrived, I asked her to send out 50 invitations of people she knew in San Diego to an event. She complained she had just arrived and didn't know that many people.

I told her about a game I played in my 20s called "Thumper." We would sit in a circle and begin a rhythm slapping our thighs going, "Categories... Names of . . . and the first person would name a category like "cars." Then we went around the circle in order and each person had to name a type of car (Chevrolet, Ford, Mercedes, etc.) until someone went temporarily blank and couldn't name one while keeping up in time with the rhythm.

The person that went blank would have to chug a whole can of beer. You can see the point of our game, but minus the beer, it's a useful tool.

I told my seminar business-builder to write down everyone she knew until she got stuck. That stuck point was her scotoma. After she got stuck, I said, "How do you know the first person on your list?"

She said the automobile repair shop. Her car had developed a problem. So, I said, "We now have our first category: Car repair, or simply cars. Does the car repair shop have anyone working there besides the person you talked to?"

"Oh yes," she said, "but I don't know them well enough to invite them." I told her to add the names to her list anyway.

I then asked, "Have you made a hair or nail appointment yet?" She had. "Are they all on your list?" You can guess what happened next. We went back and forth on categories until she had over 50 on her list.

Her subconscious knew hundreds of names and people, but her "They wouldn't be interested" or "I don't know them well enough" or "I'll look silly asking them" were scotomas screening out most of the people she already knew.

Action Step #2

Write down a description of the most emotional situation you've had in the last year. Now, write about how your viewpoint of life was shifted by that event. How did this shift in viewpoint hold you back? How did this same shift move you forward?

When you have shifted your viewpoint, it usually affects whatever you are looking at in your life and work. The first step is becoming aware of what viewpoints we have and how they are working for and against us.

An Example

When I was in my twenties, I lived in Hawaii for five years. I kept saying I just couldn't find the right woman to love, even though there were a million people in Hawaii. Perhaps 500,000 of them were of the opposite sex and maybe 50,000 in an age bracket that would work great for me, but I still couldn't find the right person.

I had a scotoma from a previous experience. I had been engaged and three days before we were to be married my fiancée walked out on me. My brain went, "I am never feeling that pain ever again."

With that conversation going on in my subconscious, I literally could not see women that might offer a great relationship with me. I would find something wrong with them so that I would not have the chance of being deeply hurt again.

When I changed my conversation to, "I am having a wildly romantic long lasting relationship whether I get hurt or not," almost out of the blue I found my wife (and have been married to her ever since). I changed my viewpoint and that opened me up to seeing what I could not see before.

> "The first thing to growth and change is to catch your-
> self being yourself."
> —Todd Demorest

Pay the Price

—Leaders know there are prices and benefits for everything

The prices—or what you have to invest or give up—are not always so obvious and, in fact, are often hidden. *If you don't know the price, it's usually higher than you want to pay.* There is no free lunch. There are prices to be paid for doing your business successfully or in making a relationship work.

There are people I know who want to be financially independent. I always ask them, "How much are you willing to pay for your financial independence?"

When I press for a specific amount of money, they sometimes squirm a bit. The problem is they want a huge return—financial independence—without having to pay for it.

Be willing to pay the price, because often times the cost of not doing something is hidden AND far more expensive.

In addition, many times we think there is a price for achieving success that isn't there or isn't as high or hard to pay as we thought. Many times I have heard people say, "I don't want to become rich or super successful because I wouldn't be able to spend any time with my family." I haven't found that to be true at all. At the same time there will be prices to be paid. There is no free lunch.

Right now, write down two things that are very important to you that you want to create. Perhaps it is a rewarding relationship, doubling the size of your business, a certain size waistline, or making a huge, positive difference in your community.

Ask yourself: How much time will this take? How uncomfortable will I need to allow myself to be? How much money will it take?

Now, tell the truth about what you are willing to pay to get that. There will be prices you are unwilling to pay. That's fine, but state clearly what you ARE willing to pay and begin to build up your willingness to pay the price. This will put you in elite company and is a giant step to achieving your result.

TAKEAWAY!

Leaders change the situation, so even after they leave, things are different than when they arrived.

Action Step#1

List 10 prices you THINK you will have to pay to reach your goal for this year. Are there any you are unwilling to pay? Interview someone who has made that level of success you are aiming for and ask that person what prices he or she paid?

Did you have any false assumptions? Now, list 10 prices you are paying for being at the level of your business you are currently at, instead of the higher level of your goal. Identify at least one price you are unwilling to continue paying.

An Example

I have a friend in a network marketing company who has not achieved the top income designation, but has sat at the second highest level for a couple years. When I asked her what it was costing to not achieve the highest level, she replied "not much." (This was why she was still #2.)

I had to press a little to get her to truly examine the real prices, but the price that caused her to move into action was when I asked her how many families were suffering because other networkers weren't going for the top level because my friend hadn't made it yet and everyone saw her as "the leader." She recognized that she was holding them back.

Action Step #2

Go back to any goal you have failed at. Now, make a commitment not to stop until you have completed it. This will build your quotient of being willing to pay the price.

An Example

There is an exercise in one of our seminars called Mount Everest. Students pick a task and must demonstrate 100 percent commitment. This is an incredibly intense exercise. It sometimes takes a couple hours and is often very uncomfortable. There is no back door; you continue until the task is complete.

It becomes an experience for people that acts as a "line in the sand," where when you say something is going to happen it will happen. It becomes an inner benchmark or reference point they rely on or recall when they hit tough times in the future.

Average people, on the other hand, approach things from the "I will do my best" perspective. That is very different from the "I WILL get it done" approach.

The willingness to pay the price is what separates the excellent from the average.

"The most important thing is to be able at any moment to sacrifice who you are for what you could become"
—Charles Dubois

Growing Your Root Structure

—Leaders are more interested in developing the root structure than the immediate visible results

There is a Chinese bamboo tree I have heard about, that when planted, you will see no growth for 90 days, then in a few short months grows 90 feet!

What it was doing prior to the explosive growth was putting down a root structure that would support its future growth.

In building the huge Sears tower in Chicago, they first went 100 feet down before they ever started building up.

Many times we invest effort in a business or relationship and we get impatient that there is no visible growth. The results we are working for just don't seem to be there. But often what's really happening is that we are changing in those hidden ways necessary to support our future results.

Growth is usually never a straight-line increase. In my experience, it's a series of intermittent increases or "growth spurts" and then plateaus.

Think of learning a sport. Most of your development occurs in leaps of getting better followed by lingering plateaus of staying at that same level (and those plateaus always seem to take too long). Near the end of your growth, it takes an incredible amount of effort and time to get those last, final, small increases in performance. It's those last small increases that separate the champions from the also-rans.

Take five minutes right now and list the ways you are investing in creating a foundation or root structure for your life and work.

Are you investing in a computer structure or accounting system that will allow you to expand? Are you investing time in extending your education in marketing, management, or technology that will allow you to grow bigger or faster?

Are you spending time developing your second layer of leadership? This is your greatest leverage. There is always a decrease in your personal production as you spend time developing other people. There needs to be a balance of both being done all the time.

Are you spending time in spiritual or inspirational studies that will give you a stronger, deeper foundation?

This week, outline a plan that will increase your root structure this year in a significant way.

TAKEAWAY!

Building a Root Structure is often invisible, but is even more important than visible growth. Invest money and time in root structures to support your desired future growth and gains. And be patient!

Action Step #1

If your income suddenly became 10 times what it is now, what would you need to know to handle that increase? What would you need to know to profitably invest that much money? What resources would you need to protect that much money? Now, develop a study program to learn those things.

An Example

As I was building my own financial portfolio, I sold a piece of property and made a $143,000 profit. At the time, this was a lot of money to me. My financial advisor (a friend who remains a friend, but no longer an advisor) told me I would either pay the tax now or pay it later, so I might as well pay it now.

Because I had not developed a financial root structure, I promptly turned approximately $65,000 over to the government. I learned my lessons "after" I should have and it was an "expensive" lesson.

If I had been doing my studying, I would have known the right questions to ask and would have sought alternatives that would have reduced that tax amount to about $5,000!

The time for you to learn about taxes and investing is "before" you make the money, not after. Some people say, "I don't want to know about that financial stuff; I just want to do my business." Then they will always be victim to the people who know the game of money.

You do not have to be "the expert" in area, but you do have to have the fundamental knowledge and continually upgrade what you know.

Action Step #2

Ask yourself: who do I want to be around and associating with in five years and who do I know who knows them that I can network with?

Take a step this week to get to know someone who knows who you want to know. Spend time building your network of people that will get you to the people you want to be around in five years. Work on your willingness to have them in your network even sooner.

Build a Rolodex of successful people. *Never let a month go by where you have not added at least one super achiever to your file of friends and associates.*

List your top three business partnerships. This is your root structure. List one thing you are doing to develop your relationship with each one of your partners.

Now list three new people who you have not spent much time with who will be future partners. What can you do to increase the value of your relationship? You must grow the roots wide and deep to grow a 90' bamboo tree.

An Example

In 2002, we spent approximately $25,000 and many staff hours developing a new web site and database that would enable us to reach more people with our seminars and that would also eliminate hours of manual internal reports.

There were lost marketing opportunities because of the time and money spent on this project. For a long time we kept duplicate records doing double entries on everything because the kinks weren't worked out yet. During that year the web site generated almost no revenue and was a cost center that looked a lot like a black hole.

We were practicing our patience through the plateau.

By 2003, automatic responders were not only saving hundreds of hours of staff time, but enabled us to market in new and unique ways. The secured credit card catalogue of products is positioned for thousands of dollars per month in sales. We created a strong and deep "digital" root structure to support explosive future growth.

> "Ninety-nine percent of who you are is invisible and untouchable."
> —R. Buckminster Fuller

Growing a Vision

—Leaders develop the vision of the organization, others, and themselves

I had lunch one day with a woman named Ann Low. Her eight-year-old daughter Landry was trying to cope with the 9-11 World Trade Center disaster. Those 3,000 people dying was such a large number for her to comprehend.

After sympathizing, Ann decided to leverage the moment in terms of instruction. She asked her daughter how many children under the age of five died every day?

Landry guessed 400,

Ann encouraged her daughter to think bigger, because this was the whole world. Landry guessed a thousand.

Ann then told her that 15,000 children under the age of five die every day. Astounded, eight-year-old Landry, committed to feeding 1,000 children.

She sat in her principal's office five days in a row before getting an appointment. When she finally got to see him, she convinced the principal to let her announce daily for eight days over the PA system that all the children in school could change the world with their spare change.

After eight days, Landry had collected a wheelbarrow full of money. It was enough to feed over 4,000 children.

If an eight-year-old can do that, what can you do in your business? Can you ignore rejection and call someone five times like Landry did as she sat in the principal's office waiting to see him for five days? Can you commit to a goal that others think is unrealistic or, based on your past, is unrealistic?

Remember that realism is for those that lack imagination. Vision is the ability to see with your imagination the potential that the physical eye cannot see. The physical eye sees facts, such as an apple seed sitting in the palm of my hand. Vision sees the potential of the tree it will become and the fruit of that tree, which has seeds and the trees of those seeds, etc.

Where in your life do you feel overwhelmed? What piece are you willing to commit to solving? Sure, 4,000 starving children being fed may not solve the whole problem, but it begins a movement of hope.

A graduate of our seminars and top marketing professional, Mark Lance, wisely states, "Take someone as far as they can see and then they can see further."

Take 10 minutes today and make a list of your goals that are outside of accumulation and in the realm of contribution or making a difference.

TAKEAWAY!
Large visions grow out of little visions. Never underestimate your ability to make a difference.

Action Step #1

Take one of your business partners and have a conversation like Ann had with her daughter. Remember, it started with something huge—3,000 people dying in one incident. It moved to something even bigger—15,000 children under the age of five dying every day. It then moved to a commitment the daughter thought she could take on—feeding 1,000 children.

With your team, that might sound like the difference a leader in your business makes in a community project or charitable cause. What if 1,000 successful people were involved? Ask yourself what you can do right now. You don't have to swallow the whole elephant right now, you just have to take one bite and start chewing.

An Example

More than 20 years ago, I interviewed Wally Amos, an international speaker and the creator of "Famous Amos" Cookies. I interviewed him because I found out he had lost the entire business of "Famous Amos" Cookies and yet, within 30 days, he had another company up, running, and making a profit. I wanted to know all about that.

During our meeting I asked him if he started with a vision of an international cookie company. Quite the contrary! His vision in the beginning was simply to have the best cookie store in Los Angeles. From that the vision grew and grew.

Action Step #2

List the biggest difference you think you make in your lifetime. Then have someone close to you give an honest evaluation if they see it the same way.

Now fantasize about what a difference that difference made in all the people touched by that person and so on. Know that you have impacted thousands. Look at all the people touched by the story of Ann and Landry.

Now, write a page in your journal on how you might make twice that difference, or, even more.

An Example

I know that this can be a difficult exercise for some people. To get you started, recall the classic holiday movie starring Jimmy Stewart, "It's a Wonderful Life." The character Stewart plays George Bailey, who is thinking of suicide and gets the chance to see what life would have been like if he had never been born.

From that perspective, take a fresh look at all the differences you've made in your life.

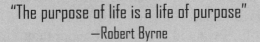

"The purpose of life is a life of purpose"
—Robert Byrne

Peanut Butter Sandwiches

—Leaders operate from being responsible, even when they don't feel like it and it doesn't seem true

A construction worker went to work every day with his black metal lunch pail under his arm. On Monday, he complained loudly about the peanut butter and jelly sandwich he had for lunch. His co-workers ignored his complaints, since it was his first day on the job.

Tuesday at lunch this same worker was even louder about how much he hated peanut butter and jelly sandwiches. There were a few rumblings from his co-workers, but they let it slide.

By Friday, after hearing him complain every day about PBJ sandwiches one of his co-workers yelled out, "Why don't you just get your wife to make you a tuna fish or Philly cheese steak sandwich or something else?"

The man looked up with a puzzled look on his face and said, "My wife? I don't have a wife. I made this myself."

What if the state of your business, your personal relationships, and your health were all simply a sandwich you made yourself? Leaders take the viewpoint that their choices create their experience, whether that is true or not.

I submit that for most people, they are living a life of a peanut butter and jelly sandwich of their own creation. Of course, it doesn't look that way to them. That's because the decisions that are creating their life are unconscious decisions instead of conscious ones.

It's what you don't know that trips you up or prevents you from producing the life you say you want. When was the last time you explored what unconscious decisions were affecting your life?

What have you bought into as reality—such as what success really means—that is merely an unconscious decision? Is there a success you are currently enjoying you think is just a coincidence or a matter of chance or lucky timing?

Explore the choices you made in setting any and all of that up. If you don't see how you create your success you will always be afraid of losing it because you won't know how to recreate it. Take one hour this week and invest it in exploring what unconscious decisions are affecting your life.

TAKEAWAY!
It is what you don't know that is stopping you. Every result in your life is a peanut butter sandwich you made for yourself.

Action Step #1

Write down one result you have in your life currently that you do not like (the size of your bank balance, the state of a relationship, the condition of your car, etc.).

Now, write down at least 10 choices you've made that set up that result; 10 thoughts, feelings, speaking or actions, which allowed that result to happen or flat out caused that result. Don't quit until you have all 10.

Now, do this same exercise with one successful result you are enjoying today.

If you don't see how you are making the great things happen you will not be able to recreate them.

Pretend your choices were at cause even if you don't believe it or feel that it isn't true.

Action Step #2

Do a seminar or hire a coach where you explore what decisions you have made about you that are unconscious. This is what our personal mastery seminar does or what a good coach can create for you.

An Example

An advanced graduate of ours (Curt Johnson) relayed a story that illustrated a peanut butter sandwich he made for himself.

Curt was struggling along with mediocre success when he took our seminars. One of his insights was that during his attendance at the Air Force Academy, his flight team had been climbing a tower in a training exercise. One girl on his team slipped and fell—from 60 feet high! Although she didn't die, it was a traumatic incident that stayed with Curt.

For years, Curt told me, he blamed the Air Force for accepting this woman into the Academy when it was obvious she lacked the standard physical requirements. He was holding that against them and he was holding that against himself as well.

What he did not see until our seminars was that although everyone saw him as a leader, Curt did not trust himself.

Curt had decided out of that incident that he couldn't trust himself. Until he saw that he just thought others believed in him falsely. What he did not know about his unconscious thinking was repeatedly holding him back from productively assuming a leadership role in anything, let alone his business.

> "One's philosophy is not best expressed in words; it is expressed in the choices one makes ... and the choices we make are ultimately our responsibility."
> —Eleanor Roosevelt

Leaders Interfere

—Leaders are bold enough to interfere in other people's lives

Do you remember studying the physicist Sir Isaac Newton in school? His first Law of Motion stated, "An object at rest tends to stay at rest and an object in motion tends to stay in motion with the same speed and in the same direction unless acted upon by an outside force."

Objects (and you and I are "objects") tend to keep on doing what they're doing. In fact, it's the natural tendency of objects and people to resist changes in their state of motion. This tendency to resist changes in their state of motion is described as "inertia."

What has been the direction of your business? If your business continues on its current path for a year will you be happy? What has been the direction of your family life? Will you be satisfied if it maintains its current course for another year?

Leaders are the force in other people's lives that alter the direction that life is taking. *A positive leader interferes in other people's lives and causes them to do what they otherwise would not do toward what is important to them.*

That's service. If leaders interfere for their own purpose, then it's manipulation. You have to know what the other person wants in order to interfere and be of service. Are you bold enough to interfere?

Whose life can you impact this week by finding out what they want and then be bold enough to cause them to do what they would not have done on their own? Commit to doing that.

TAKEAWAY!

Servant leadership requires caring enough to interfere, but doing so by giving what is wanted and needed not what we want to give.

Action Step #1

Ask several business partners or members of your team what they want to achieve this week. Now commit yourself to actions that will "interfere" in their lives to support them to accomplish their goal.

Yes, it's uncomfortable. You have to be more committed to what they want for themselves than what they think of you in the moment. You cannot lead people whose approval you need. This might be as simple as sitting with them until they make a certain call, forcing them to do a presentation when they don't feel they are ready for yet, or requiring an accountability call from the person each day after they have completed a challenging task. There are many ways you can interfere to cause powerful, productive action.

An Example

Early in John Milton Fogg's career in network marketing, his upline sponsor made him do a five-minute introduction of himself at his first meeting. The next meeting, John's sponsor had him do 10 minutes on the products. The next meeting, he had him do 10 minutes on the opportunity. Right before the very next meeting, he called John to say he was unavoidably detained and John would have to do the whole presentation himself.

John said, "No way! I'm not ready!" His sponsor said he couldn't be there and told John to do the best he could. John later found out that this was what his sponsor always did. It was his way of interfering to cause his new reps to do what they otherwise would not do towards what mattered to them and their success in the business.

Action Step #2

Find a seminar that will alter your path before you need to. This could be one of our seminars at Klemmer & Associates or another you're attracted to, but pick some seminar that will challenge and change your thinking. Rarely if ever does that happen without the influence of an outside force. Perhaps it's taking a trip to a third world country or to a really depressed neighborhood near you and being of service. (Note: Journal about any changes you notice in your life and work.)

An Example

Our Personal Mastery, Advanced Leadership, and Heart of the Samurai seminars are often a force that creates an organization or a person's life going in a new, accelerated, more successful direction.

Good leaders are proactive about creating such forces in their own life or the life of their organization. Average people wait for the force to hit them.

Patrick Dean is one of our advanced leadership facilitators. Among other things, he is an excellent surfer. I am not a good surfer. If and when I finally get up on the board, I ride it all the way to the end. You eat a lot of sand that way.

A good surfer like Patrick is off the wave looking for the next one long before that wave ends. Good businesses are the same way. They are looking for a new product or new marketing long before their current good one is obsolete.

This week, plan something in the next 90 days that will be that outside force causing your life or that of your organization to go in a new direction even if the one you have currently is very successful direction.

"None of us has gotten where we are solely by pulling ourselves up by our own bootstraps. We got here because somebody ... bent down and helped us."
—Thurgood Marshall

Dispelling Discouragement

—Leaders are vigilant about not letting discouragement into people's lives

There's an old story about the devil having a "Going Out of Business" sale. Now, I think you'll agree that's a pretty amazing prospect.

He had this huge room filled with everything he ever owned or used to do his work and the prices were displayed openly on every item.

In the very center of the room was a small podium and the tiniest item in the room was there on top. The price on the tag was by far the highest, most expensive in the whole room.

Someone asked the devil, "What is that on the podium that is so small and yet is the most expensive item you have?"

The devil said it was "discouragement" and it was the most expensive because with that he didn't need anything else to do his work.

Think about that. Be vigilant about not letting discouragement into your life anywhere: not for your business, not for your health, not for the state of your relationships, etc.

Sometimes we think we have to listen to other people's negativity to be a nice person. DON'T LISTEN! And don't allow them to pollute your mind and your coworkers or family's mind either. It brings discouragement.

Leaders control the conversation and will end a discussion or change the topic if necessary. Leaders will stop someone from complaining if the person is complaining to someone else who cannot do anything about it.

Leaders will be proactive at dispelling discouragement in other people's lives, especially family, partners, or team at work. Leaders will seek out someone who is discouraged and give them encouragement or assist them in focusing on what is working, what's right.

What can you do today to dispel discouragement in someone else's life?

Make a list of three people you will say or do something for this week to dispel discouragement out of their life. Commit to doing that.

TAKEAWAY!

Leaders dispel discouragement. Leaders control the conversation and keep it positive and constructive.

Action Step #1

Find a couple people who are discouraged and make a massive infusion of encouragement into their life. Let them know about a similar experience or setback you've had or about someone you know who has and what positive changes came out of it.

Simply share your enthusiasm and shift their focus to what works and the possibilities.

Write a simple postcard to 10 people telling them the one thing you admire most about them and that you believe that quality will be the reason for their success. As Winston

Churchill said, "Success is the ability to go from failure to failure without losing your enthusiasm."

An Example

About two years ago I got an email that asked, "Are you the Brian Klemmer that served in the 25th Infantry division as an officer in the 1/21st Battalion in the early 70's?"

I replied, "Yes I am."

He said, "You probably don't remember me, my name is (withheld for confidentiality), but if you do remember, it's because you busted me for drugs. You made me get my GED (high school equivalency diploma) and I fought you kicking and screaming.

I'm writing to let you know how appreciative I am. I am sitting here in a good job and my whole life is different because you cared about me more than I cared about myself."

I have to tell you that didn't just make my day. It made my year! I think about that letter every time I do a seminar and someone is being resistant or negative.

Action Step #2

Now, interview a very successful person in any field. Ask what was their biggest setback and what one or two things did they do that helped them overcome it. That will dispel your discouragement.

An Example

Who is this famous "failure"? He failed as a businessman (storekeeper). He failed as a farmer (he despised this work). His sweetheart died. He had a nervous breakdown. He failed in his first attempt to obtain political office.

He was elected to the legislature, but he failed when he sought the office of speaker. He failed in his first attempt to go to Congress. He failed when he sought the appointment to the United States Land Office. He failed when he ran for the United States Senate. He failed when friends sought for him the nomination for the Vice-Presidency.

And, in 1860, Abraham Lincoln was elected president of the United States of America.

"No matter how busy you are, you must take time to make the other person feel important."
—Mary Kay Ash

Momentum and Massive Action

—Leaders create the kind of action that leads to building lasting momentum

Have you ever watched a satellite launch? Do you know that sometimes even when the satellite is perfectly on target they will blow it up?

Imagine that! A perfectly good (and incredibly expensive) satellite and it's precisely on course and they blow it up? Why?

The reason is that there is a certain speed it takes to break out of the earth's orbit. That's called "escape velocity." I believe it is in the neighborhood of 25,000 miles per hour. If the satellite has not reached that critical speed, then even though it's on course it won't break out of the earth's orbit. The scientists blow it up so it won't fall back to earth, hurt people, and do damage.

I believe our business and personal life is much the same. People need to create a critical speed so they can break through to the next level. One way to do that is MASSIVE action.

You identify a period of time like a month or six months. You commit to have an extra-ordinary amount of action. It is not a pace you can keep up forever. *Its purpose is to create breakthrough momentum.*

Did you know a train that is stopped can have a small six-inch block of steel on the track and that alone can prevent it from moving, though the locomotive weighs 40 tons or more! Yet, that same train moving with a momentum of 50 miles per hour will run right through a tractor-trailer like it was paper.

Momentum can overcome many problems that would otherwise keep you stuck. It is more effective to focus on building momentum and letting momentum overcome the obstacle you face, rather than focusing directly on the obstacle.

What area of your life are you willing to create momentum in? What period of time are you willing to commit to massive action? Make a list of the actions you will take, and start today.

TAKEAWAY!
Focus on building momentum instead of directly over coming an obstacle. MASSIVE action is one powerful way to create momentum.

Action Step #1

Think of an ordinary problem you have. List 10 things you can do in other areas of your life to build momentum to overcome that problem that have nothing to do with the problem itself.

An Example

Let's say your problem is work related. What momentum could you gain by making time to do some physical exercise? How about putting in some needed relaxation? Or study? Every success in one part of your life will add momentum to other areas even when they do not seem related at all.

Action Step #2

Now, think of your biggest problem. What momentum can you focus on building through massive action to overcome that obstacle? Write down five things that will create that momentum.

If you get stuck thinking of five items, you can form accountability partnerships or a mastermind group and brainstorm with them until you not only have five things, but you make an agreement with your partners as to what specific actions you will do this week to build momentum.

An Example

Young Glenn Cunningham used to run to the little country schoolhouse every morning and start the wood stove. He loved to run more than any thing and the money he earned helped his family.

One day the teacher and some students arrived to see the schoolhouse engulfed in flames. The fuel oil used to start the fire had ignited the entire building. They pulled Glenn out of the inferno and rushed him to the hospital. He was so badly burned the doctors expected him to die within hours.

To the amazement of everyone, Glenn survived. But it was clear he would never walk, much less run, again. He had no motor ability in his legs and they were severely burned, damaged beyond repair.

Everyday his mother would massage his shriveled legs with oil, to ease the pain and try to bring some life back into them. But there was no feeling, no movement, nothing.

In time, through his mother's unceasing care, Glen developed enough strength to go outside in a wheel chair. One day, he threw himself from the chair and dragged his body across the yard, pulling himself up on the white picket fence. Hand over hand, picket by picket, he dragged himself along the fence. He was determined he would walk again. Every day, day after day, Glen would drag himself all around the fence. He wore a path in the grass in the yard inside the fence.

Through his mother's massages and truly super-human effort and iron will, Glen began to stand, then walk and finally to run. And not just to run, but to run faster than any human being had before.

For three years, from 1932 to 1934, he won the Big Six indoor track titles and was again at the Olympics in 1936 (he'd also competed in 1932). In 1938, Glen Cunningham became the world's fastest miler as he set a new record at Dartmouth College. That same year he also received a doctorate degree from New York University.

By simply going outside, each day, every day in a wheel chair—nothing spectacular, but it got the momentum going—Glen Cunningham was finally able to cast aside his circumstances and achieve greatness.

> "It is even better to act quickly and err than to hesitate until the time of action is past."
> —Karl Von Clausewitz

Leadership Is Sales

—Leaders understand that sales is the most important skill in being successful as a leader

Do you have a negative reaction to sales? Many people do. Why is it people love to buy, but hate to be sold? Well, guess what? Everyone is in sales—EVERYONE!

Have you ever gone out on a date? That was sales. You sold the other person on asking you out OR you sold him or her on saying, "Yes" to you.

Have you ever comforted a person who was feeling sad or bad? That was sales. You were selling them on feeling different and better.

Have you ever gotten married? That was a huge sale! (By the way, in my viewpoint the biggest problem in most marriages today is the same as most other sales: We forget to service what we sold!)

Sales is communicating in such a way that you cause action. Let me repeat that: Sales is communicating in such a way that you cause action.

That's very different than just informing or educating people. And it is certainly not jamming something down someone's throat they don't want. That doesn't cause positive productive action—it causes resistance!

It could be argued (and I do) that sales is the single most important skill to learn to be successful in life. If you want your children to study and do well in school, you must know how to sell. They will not study just because you tell them to.

Every interaction between two people is really a sales situation. There will always be a buyer and a seller. What have other people been selling you, your friends, family members, and business associates? Leaders are good at sales and great leaders are great at sales.

Here is a sales formula that works. If you follow it, you will get more of what you want and assist others in getting what they want as well: WANT > PROBLEM > SOLUTION.

Find out what the person WANTS. Have them tell you what their PROBLEM is in getting it. Then, you can offer your SOLUTION to solve that problem.

It must be done in that order. Most people try to go out of order and they fail to make the sale. They present their solution first, whether it is in their business or role as a parent. Consequently, they're usually not successful.

Pick one area of your life whether it is coaching a business partner, dating, or parenting. Commit to following the Want > Problem > Solution for the week. Notice how much more effective you are at "sales."

TAKEAWAY!

A sale is not something you pursue, it's what happens to you while you are immersed in serving your customer.

Action Step #1

Enroll your son or daughter (or other family member or friend) in helping you complete a personal project, such as something around the house using the Want > Problem > Solution formula.

An Example

Let's say *you* want the dishes done. Find out what *they* want. Perhaps your teenager wants a later curfew. Ask what their problem is in getting it. They reply you won't let them. You then ask if they are interested in a solution. They reply yes. You now come back with the solution. You say if they do the dishes for a month without you having to remind them they can have an hour later curfew as long as they come home on time.

Action Step #2

Look around the world today and pick out at least one situation that's important to you. It could be something to do with the environment, education, or a social ill you see needs a cure. Choose something you want to change.

Now, write down the Want > Problem > Solution as you see it. Don't limit any part of the formula by what you think is possible right now.

Once you've completed writing your sales formula, share that with enough other people until you've sold your idea to at least two other people.

"The aim of marketing is to know and understand the customer so well the product or service fits him and sells itself."

—Peter Drucker

David and Goliath
—Leaders welcome resistance

Nothing great becomes great without overcoming great resistance. Christianity did not become great during the time of Christ. It became great when the Christians had to overcome persecution and being eaten by the lions. The Jewish faith was the same. Any country is the same. Any organization is the same. So is a person.

Overcoming resistance is how people and their organizations become what they need to become in order to be great. The only way you get muscles is by lifting weights. Resistance is simply the weights.

That's a very different perspective on resistance than the average person has. The average person doesn't want any resistance in his or her life. They resist resistance.

Did you ever hear, "What you resist persists?"

Your resistance to an outside resistance makes the problem worse. Most people have a deep-seated belief they must resist in order to maintain control, but that always backfires.

So what resistance are you experiencing in your life? Can you get excited about that as the very thing you need to build your muscles for greatness?

It's the story of David and Goliath. Goliath was the best thing to happen to David. Without overcoming Goliath, David could not have become King. No one would have known about him. He would not have developed certain attributes that allowed him later to rule the kingdom.

Most people want to be kings and queens, but they never want to have to fight a Goliath.

Maybe the resistance you are experiencing is an economic downturn. Perhaps it is a spouse not supportive of the work you do. Maybe it is some employees who are resisting a new direction you are taking your department or the whole company. Perhaps you're in sales and prospects are resisting your price. Maybe you have children who resist you.

Non-resistance on your part to outside resistance does not mean you throw your hands up in resignation. It is an acknowledgment of how things are, which frees you up to have an effective response.

There are two kinds of resistance: *external* and your own *internal* resistance. I'm speaking here of a leader's ability to embrace outside resistance as a positive step in growth. Re-frame external resistance as simply part of the necessary steps you're taking in becoming great.

(If you would like to hear an unusual version of David and Goliath and the seven keys on how he overcame resistance, order it at www.klemmer.com.)

TAKEAWAY!

If you want an extra-ordinary life, then you must face extra-ordinary resistance. Welcome resistance instead of resisting it or looking to minimize the amount of resistance you face.

Action Step #1

What was the last major resistance you faced or are facing? What was the lesson you learned that made you stronger?

Place a stone (like the one David used in his sling to slay Goliath) on your desk where you work to remind yourself that resistance is good!

Action Step #2

Read a story this week on someone who has overcome resistance. Some suggested biographies are Abraham Lincoln, Helen Keller, Donald Trump, or Winston Churchill. Write down three things they did that you can also do.

An Example

I come from a background where everyone in my family went to college. It was expected. My wife's family is very successful, but no one graduated from college so they didn't have the same value.

Our oldest son resisted school. He flat out didn't like it and for years I resisted that. The result was that our relationship wasn't very good. I was trying to change him instead of work with what I had.

I thought there was something wrong with him and the situation. I finally stopped resisting. It wasn't working. I asked myself, "What could I do and where could I take this situation that would be good?" I started by simply listening to him. Then, I was honest with my own fears.

The first good thing that came out of it was a great relationship with my son. Then, it became an exploration of what he could do without a college education.

Interestingly enough, one of the turns the journey took was that he entered college and graduated from San Francisco State at the age of 24. He worked for me for a while, which never would have happened before, and then he went on to pursue his career.

My overcoming my resistance not only made me a better parent with my other children, but a better CEO of our company.

Life is not so threatening when what used to be a threat is now a friend.

"One man with courage makes a majority"
—Andrew Jackson

Change or Crash
—Leaders make change their lifestyle

If you don't change, crashing is certain. This is true in business, marriage, and any other pursuit. The world is a constantly changing road, so if you don't continually adjust the steering wheel you will eventually crash.

Leaders make change their lifestyle. They practice changing until they are comfortable with it and it becomes a habit. Learn what to change and what not to change. Control the direction and speed of change.

It has been said that Socrates was instructing his star pupil Plato about the subject of change. He explained that everything began at a point of energy and went through a phase where it expanded and got bigger. He called this phase growth.

Then things went through a period where nothing changed, which he called stability. Then it went through another phase where it shrank or decreased until it returned to the original point of energy. Socrates called this last phase decay.

Plato is reported to have pondered this awhile and then returned to disagree with his mentor. He said that there are only two phases, not three. The two phases were growth and decay. Plato argued that stability is an illusion and that things are always either growing or decaying.

If you look at a common table, it is in slow decay. The varnish or finish slows the decay down, while fire would speed it up. You can control the speed of change and the direction of change, but not whether things will change.

We want to believe in stability because it gives the illusion of security, safety and comfort. It allows us to avoid action. Pretend there is no such thing as stability. Then ask yourself: Is my business growing or decaying? Are my significant relationships growing or decaying? Is my health growing or decaying? Is my spiritual nature growing or decaying? What changes are occurring around me that I am resisting? What actions am I compelled to take now?

(My book, *When Good Intentions Run Smack Into Reality* covers this in greater detail.) Commit to doing something different each day this week and record your reactions to change.

TAKEAWAY!

Change is a requirement for success. Develop an appetite for change and you will automatically be in the top 5%.

Action Step #1

Most everyone has a dominant hand: right or left. Starting today, and for this entire week, brush your teeth with your opposite hand. Notice your thoughts and feelings day-by-day and write them down.

Action Step #2

Get a partner. Look at how each of you is dressed. Now, turn back to back and individually make two or three changes in how you are dressed.

Turn back facing each other and see how many of the other person's changes you are aware of. Repeat this three times. Write down the thoughts and feelings you experience around change.

An Example

In the last few years, the stock market has gone through a pretty wild boom and bust cycle. What's so interesting is that when the stock market was declining, most of the news was negative. Almost nowhere in the normal news media did you hear it referred to simply as what was and how to take advantage of it.

I put myself on a track of learning about puts and calls and how to take advantage of a market in decline. I began to learn that money can be earned many times even faster in a downward market. It simply required a different strategy. It was learning to ride the river in the direction it was going.

Like sailing a boat, instead of complaining about the wind, you learn to use the wind's power to take you in the direction you want to go.

"In times of change learners inherit the earth while learned find themselves beautifully equipped to deal with a world that no longer exists"
—Eric Hoffer

Give First

—Leaders systematically give what they want to receive

Imagine you are lying in a sleeping bag inside a log cabin with the snow coming down outside. As you first open your eyes, all that's sticking out of your sleeping bag is your eyes and nose because it is SO cold.

You realize the reason it's so cold is that there is no fire in the wood stove. In fact, you become aware there's no wood inside the cabin! You have A PROBLEM.

Now, you try and get very creative and you tell the stove, "Look, if you will just warm me up a little, then I'll gladly run outside and get you some wood."

Silly, yet how much of our lives do we live that way? We say to our spouse, "Spend more time with me and I will love you more." And your mate is saying back to you, "Love me more and I will spend more time with you." The stove won't heat up until you put wood into it!

In many businesses, employees are saying, "Pay me more and I will work harder." Management is saying, "Work harder and I will pay you more." Again, the stove won't heat up until you put wood into it.

Become a giving maniac. Be on a mission to give first, even when you don't see how it will come back to you.

This week, when you go to work, consciously decide how to give to the receptionist, your boss, someone out in the field, or someone in another department. Try giving simply because you have decided to be a giver and see what happens. The reasons for giving are many.

Also, it is plain FUN to give. Think about the last time you gave and how it felt. It's not only fun, it's fulfilling. Giving has other practical benefits. You give and it sometimes comes back from that person. But other times it comes back from some other source.

For many people, when the giving does not come back from the person or organization they gave to, they falsely conclude that giving does not pay.

I am a huge believer in tithing (giving 10 percent of everything you earn back to God). Besides the spiritual lessons, in a very practical way this convinces your sub-conscious of the abundance that is out there in the world.

Giving builds loyalty in the relationships you have. We are prevented from giving first because of three factors:

- Our pride says that someone doesn't really deserve it.
- Our viewpoint of scarcity that there is not enough to go around or will be left for us.
- Our self-centered point of view.

It always amazes me that when people complain about not having enough time and I tell them to give some time away, they resist. They insist they do not have enough time and I insist they give some away.

The perceived need for survival blinds us receiving from many, many sources.

TAKEAWAY!

If you want something, then give it first. Receiving does not necessarily come from the same place to which you have given.

Action Step #1

What is it you lack most: Time? Money? Control? Recognition? Begin a systemized way of giving what you lack on a regular basis. You want a "system," not a random act of giving, because repetition will build and create more and more momentum.

Action Step #2

Pick someone you want to receive something from. Now, find out what it is that they want and give that to them. Many times we give what we want to give, missing the mark widely from what it is they want to be given.

An Example

Several years ago, we had done a few classes for a network marketing company with their distributors. As usual, those men and women became not just clients, but good friends we cared about.

One day I got a call from a director in the company. He shared with me that they had some severe challenges going on. They had gone public at about $8 a share, and the stock price had dropped to $1. There was conflict and even lawsuits being threatened.

He said he knew of our sales training, but asked if I also did conflict resolution. I said yes, but not directly. I told him to put the senior management in a room along with the key "upset" distributors and I would fly in at my own expense and spend a day with them and then we'd see what developed.

I gave freely of my time and expertise. The day turned out very well, and it led to close to a million dollars in business for us with that company.

Have I given and not had it come back from the same company or person? Sure, but in some way from some where, it always comes back.

"My father was a successful businessman. When he died no one remembered him for his skill at reading the markets. The remembered him for the favors he did"
—Rabbi Harold Kushner

The Servant Leader

—Leaders are driven by being of service to people

Why should you make more money? Because you can be a bigger blessing to more people. Leaders are driven by being of service to people.

Without money you can offer your compassion and encouragement, but with money you can do more—so much more. You can make a difference.

Do you know the story of the good Samaritan in the Bible? Regardless of your religious persuasion, it's a great story I recommend you read (Luke 10:30-36).

Most people think of it as a story of compassion, because two people passed by a hurt man on the road without helping him. One felt he had more important things to do and the other was afraid of getting involved.

But the third person, the Samaritan, took him to an inn and asked the innkeeper to take care of him for a month. He also gave the innkeeper enough coins to take care of the man and told him that if it weren't enough, he'd give him more when he came back in 30 days.

How many innkeepers do you think would have taken the hurt man on for no cash? The only reason the Samaritan could do what he did was because he had the money.

When people tell me they do not care about making more money, I shock them by telling them, "That is the most selfish thing I have ever heard!"

I wait until they ask why and I explain that to take care of themselves is easy to do. It does not require much money. But to truly care for all those others who need help takes courage and compassion . . . and more money! *"If you don't want more money, then you obviously only care about yourself or a very limited number of people."*

How big a blessing do you want to be to others? Most people live in a world of indifference because they are afraid they are incapable of making a difference. Allow yourself to see the needs of the world so that you have the need to create enormous amounts of cash.

Commit this week to making and giving away more money than you ever have before.

TAKEAWAY!

The purpose of making money is to be a bigger blessing to more people. The way you use money describes your true value system.

Action Step #1

Pull out your checkbook. Look at the last three months. Outside of bills and birthdays, how much money have you spent on other people?

An Example

My friend John is what's known as a big tipper. Even when John has been close to broke—and he has—he hands out five-dollar bills to skycaps at airports and bellhops. He always tips serving people 20 percent and usually more.

John says he's just helping the people who are helping him. Win-win.

Action Step #2

Get out of your daily routine and expose yourself to the needs of others. Visit a children's hospital and talk, not just to the children, but to the parents and administrators as to how it is being paid for.

Go to a homeless shelter and ask them what they could do if they had $10,000 more a month. Now, come up with two or three things you could do to make sure they get that money.

An Example

I have another friend named Azim Khamiza. His 19-year-old only son was shot and killed by a 13-year-old gangster.

His son was delivering pizza as a way to work through school and a gang held him up. When he refused to give up the pizza, the 13-year-old was ordered to kill him.

Until I met Azim, my mind didn't even want to think of these kinds of occurrences. Violence seemed far away from me. Yet, after meeting Azim, I was exposed to how prevalent violence is with many of our youth.

Azim and the guardian of his son's killer, Plez Felix, formed the TKF Foundation to end violence among youth. In one year alone our Klemmer & Associates Heart of the Samurai graduates pledged over 1 million dollars for TKF (www.TKF.org).

In one sense that is great, but in another sense it is but a drop in the bucket as to what needs to be done. For a mere 30 dollars a child they make a real statistically significant difference on steering youth away from violence.

It requires courage to open up to the need and allowing oneself to be compelled to do something about it.

"Life's most persistent and urgent question is 'what are you doing for others?'"
—Martin Luther King Jr

Facts Are Not Meanings

—Leaders recognize that facts do not mean any one thing

Your brain can store 100 trillion facts. Your mind can handle 15,000 decisions a second. You can smell 10,000 different odors. Your touch can detect a 1/25,000 of an inch of difference. You can taste one part quinine in 2 million parts water.

So, why is it you don't feel special or capable? **What an absurd notion!** I suggest that something happened and you decided you were not important or special. Write two words down: FACT and MEANING.

Facts are experiences, feelings we've had, while **meaning** is the "interpretation" we put to that experience or feeling.

A friend of mine wanted a doll when she was very young. Her father would not get it for her. That's a fact. It's something that really happened. Then she put a meaning to it. She decided she wasn't worth it. If she was really worth it, her dad would have bought the $10 doll.

Can you think of another meaning she could have put to that very same fact? Sure you can, such as, "We can't afford it, or Dad does not love me." Now, think of one or two more meanings.

The point is, we make up meanings for everything that happens in life. Begin to realize that you are making the meanings up. **Facts are not meanings!** They are two separate things.

Most people take meanings to be true and believe there could be no other meaning. This is huge! Leaders, on the other hand, recognize that facts do not mean any one thing.

If you are in sales, what do you make the word "No" mean? Suppose it meant something other than the person wasn't interested?

If you have a boss who did not return a phone call, what did you make that mean? What if you picked the wrong meaning?

What happened where you decided you weren't special? What else could you make that same experience mean that would help you in living the life you want? It may not mean that, but at least pick meanings that support you in the direction you want to go in life.

When young students completely flunk a test, they invariably make it mean that they are slow, stupid, a failure, or something similar. It doesn't mean that.

For many years I would go into schools and in 10 minutes have the children memorize all the colonies in the order they signed the constitution. Then I would have a child stand up who I knew was flunking. I would get them to give me the first 13 colonies—in the order they signed the constitution! They always got it right.

Then they would do it backwards. They'd go cross-eyed. They had a mental melt down of sorts, because now they were thinking they were a genius.

It didn't really mean that, but I would rather they thought they were a genius, because that changed their study habits, how they listened, how they performed on tests—and most importantly, what they thought about themselves.

TAKEAWAY!
You are special, not because of anything you have done. It is simply so. Facts in and of themselves do not have any inherent meaning.

Action Step #1

This week, pretend you are very special. Live as if you were very unique, valuable, and special. Talk with a tone of voice as if you were special. Talk to the people you would normally talk to if you were special.

Action Step #2

Write down your most vivid memory as a child. Then, write down everything you made that mean about you or life. What do you see?

An Example

My friend, Bob Harrison, and I were both speaking at a large convention in Sweden. He shared something personal with me he has said is okay for me to share with you.

His childhood sweetheart and wife of 37 years had died a little over a year before. He had started dating again and some of his friends felt that it was too early to date and that could mean he had not cared as deeply for his wife as they had thought.

Bob had loved his wife dearly and was hurt by their reactions. I told him not to be upset and showed him why not with my explanation about fact-and-meaning.

The fact he was dating again did not necessarily mean that he had not had deep feelings for her. It could mean that being married to her was such a wonderful experience that he greatly missed that kind of relationship. My example helped to relieve his anxiety.

Months later Bob told me a story that is a very funny example of fact vs meaning. Bob is a motivational speaker and he's in front of crowds of

10,000 and more regularly (www.increase.org). One occasion he was teaching on increase to a seminar group. He noticed one individual in the audience who just didn't seem to be interested in what he was saying. The man just sat there with his eyes closed and was not taking any notes of Bob's presentation. Bob determined that he was going to get this man to be attentive. He walked across the stage to a section of the crowd that was really into his presentation. He got himself all charged up and went back over to the guy who had his eyes closed.

Still no reaction! He went back to the highly motivated section again, talked with them and then returned to the other side to find the man STILL had his eyes closed.

About the fifth time of going over to the man with his eyes closed, Bob went a bit further to that side and got closer to the man. It was then that he noticed something in the aisle next to the man . . . a seeing eye dog. It wasn't that the man wasn't motivated and not enjoying the teaching. He was blind!

Bob said, "Never again will I be so quick to make a fact mean something."

> "The truth is more important than the facts"
> —Frank Lloyd Wright

Acting in the Face of Fear

—Leaders train themselves to be bold in the face of fear

A firefighter who was fighting the oil fires at the end of the Persian Gulf War commented, "A man that is afraid can't think."

Now, I've always maintained that if you were not afraid, then you were smoking something funny and living in fantasyland.

Here's how I see both those statements as valid, instead of an "either or." We live in a scary world. With 9-11 and terrorism there is uncertainty. If you have children, no matter where you live, your child is exposed to illegal drugs at an early age. A business setback, a lost job, a serious illness, a relationship reversal can come out of nowhere at anytime.

Fighting an oil fire is dangerous business. That's reality. So is living life. To not be afraid is foolish.

At the same time, the fear does not have to determine your actions. When fear is what you think about or it is in control of your decision making process, then you are doomed. That's what the oil fighter was addressing. It's natural to be afraid of the fire, but if that controls you then you are ineffective.

Boldness is a must. It is one of the 10 traits that we deal with in developing what we call the compassionate samurai program. Much like the firefighter in the Persian Gulf, it must be practiced.

Many people go to seminars or read books looking for an instant cure. You can have a dramatic change. But to sustain real mastery, it must be practiced.

Leaders train themselves to be bold in the face of fear. There is fear of rejection, fear of being wrong, fear of not mattering, fear of physical pain or death, and fear of not looking good. What action can you commit to once a week for the next three months to practice action in the face of one of those particular fears?

It might be the practice of having open, honest, vulnerable communication. It might be the practice of tithing in the face of scarcity around money.

It might be the practice of investing money regularly despite uncertain times. That's the whole idea of dollar cost averaging. You invest the same amount of money regularly. It takes fear and greed out of the equation.

If you do not have a specific consistent practice, the odds are you will not do it.

TAKEAWAY!

Learn to be comfortable with being uncomfortable. Mastery is a result of practicing over time to correct unwanted behaviors and establish positive new ones.

Action Step #1

Like a pilot practicing pulling his plane out of stalls, practice courage in the face of fear. Every day this week, find a situation where you are fearful of saying something to someone and say it.

Do not pick situations where your job, relationship, or life is at stake. Perhaps it is speaking out in a management meeting, telling someone that you love them, or simply saying "No" to someone when you do not want to do something but feel pressure to say "Yes."

Action Step #2

Find a physical activity that seems scary, but where the fear is an illusion. This could be a roller coaster ride or bungee jump at an amusement park, take lessons and tandem jump from an airplane, or force yourself to dance if you are embarrassed.

An Example

Mother Teresa had the following piece, which is all about being bold and acting in the face of fear, engraved on her children's home in Calcutta. It's called "Anyway."

People are often unreasonable, illogical, and self-centered; Forgive them anyway.

If you are kind, people may accuse you of selfish, ulterior motives; Be kind anyway.

If you are successful, you will win some false friends and some true enemies; Succeed anyway.

If you are honest and frank, people may cheat you; Be honest and frank anyway.

What you spend years building, someone could destroy overnight; Build anyway.

If you find serenity and happiness, they may be jealous; Be happy anyway.

The good you do today, people will often forget tomorrow; Do good anyway.

Give the world the best you have, and it may never be enough; Give the world the best you've got anyway.

You see, in the final analysis, it is between you and God; It was never between you and them anyway.

"Never take counsel of your fears"
—Andrew Jackson

Play a Really Big Game
—Leaders have a plan for 25, 50, 100, and even 500 years

My mentor once asked me for my life plan. I didn't have one. He made me go home and not come back to work until I had my plan down on paper.

After a few days I returned to work and handed him several pages. He asked me why my life plan only went 50 years? (At the time I was 27 and I figured that was a pretty good life plan.) He said, "Don't you get anything?"

I was thoroughly confused. He asked, "Why set goals that last only as long as the body?"

He said, "Don't you realize you are a spiritual being who HAS a body? And, if that's true, why not set 500 year goals for what will be going on in the world as a result of when you had a body."

"At the least," he continued, "set 100 years goals, figuring that you will leave a wake on this company, your family, your community and your church much like a boat leaves a wake behind in the water when it passes."

How big a game do you want to play? You can be average, like most people, and not even set goals at all, or at best have New Year's resolutions.

You can set yourself apart by having a plan that lasts as long as your think your body will. Or you can be a visionary and play a really big game. It's your choice.

Do you have the courage to take one hour this week and set a 500-year goal, a couple 300-year goals, a handful of 100-year goals, and a few more 50-year goals?

Don't be afraid. You can change them. In fact, you most likely will. The biggest benefit you'll get is that you are now beginning to take a very long view of your life on earth instead of being myopic and limiting your contribution.

> ## TAKEAWAY!
> Look for the long view. Ask yourself, "Will this really matter five years from now? Knowing your purpose is a longer view than simply having a goal.

Action Step #1

Write a page on what you want to be remembered for seven generations from now.

Action Step #2

Write three: 500-year goals, 100-year goals, 50-year goals, 25-year goals, 5-year goals, and 1-year goals.

An Example

There was a well-known study of the Harvard University class of '53. In this study, the researchers revealed that only 10 percent of the students had established any goals at all, and that only three percent of the men and women in that class had written their goals down on paper.

Twenty years later, the researchers again interviewed those very same former class members. They were involved in their careers and had families now.

The three percent who two decades earlier had written down their goals were now worth more in economic terms than the entire remaining 97 percent of the class combined!

Of course financial success isn't everything, but this study clearly shows the results of writing down your goals.

Now, imagine the results you'll achieve by writing down your goals for 25, 50, 100, even 500 years!

> "Men do less than they ought, unless they do all that they can."
> —Thomas Carlyle

Chasing Rabbits

—Leaders do not get distracted from their purpose

Are rabbits dangerous? A farmer went to town in his wagon and had his dog running alongside. Every few hundred yards the dog would take off chasing a rabbit into the woods. Then, a few minutes later, he'd join back up with the wagon.

Over and over this happened. When the farmer finished the six-mile trip in to town, one storekeeper looked at the dog that was panting heavily, staggering, barely able to walk and commented that must have been a really long, hard trip. "Look," he said. "It darn near killed your dog."

The farmer replied, "It wasn't the trip that almost killed my dog. It was the rabbits."

Think about that. Have you been having a hard time with your business? What rabbits have you been chasing? Perhaps you allowed an unexpected phone call to take you on a side-trip that wasted 10 minutes, and got you no further progress toward your main goal for the day. Perhaps you got hung up doing paperwork that really didn't benefit the bottom line.

Many people think they work hard because they have lots of activities, but very few of them really are those key activities that generate revenue.

I have heard that salespeople spend only 30 percent of their time actually in front of a potential customer. How productive is that?

What if you could shift 10 percent of your time to revenue generating activities, such as actually being in front of the customer asking do they want your product?

Maybe you allowed yourself to be upset with a family member and got caught up in what we refer to in our Personal Mastery Seminars as the 3Rs: Resentment, Resistance, Revenge. A half-hour of precious quality time after work was wasted instead of creating the exciting relationship you both wanted.

For the next week, make a list at the end of each day of all the rabbits you chased. Estimate how much time and energy it cost you. Cut a picture out of a magazine of a rabbit and put it on your desk.

Commit to not chasing rabbits. It's not what you are willing to do that determines your success, it's what you are not willing to do.

TAKEAWAY!

Distractions are killer rabbits. They seem harmless, but they kill your goals as sure as anything else.

Action Step #1

Buy a little rabbit figurine and put it on your desk or on your kitchen counter where you will see it frequently. At the end of every day this week, write one page listing any and all rabbits you chased that day. Then write down what you could have done with that time.

Action Step #2

Make a list of five key activities that generate the most productivity and that have the biggest pay off for you in your job. Your job could be as a manager, a parent, a clerk, a salesperson, or a student. Commit to doing more of those as well as less chasing rabbits.

An Example

Technology is great. So many of the advances we have today have helped us do more in less time, yet some of the advantages turn out to like chasing rabbits.

One of my favorite examples is e-mail. Every 15 minutes my computer can automatically send and receive my e-mail. I don't have to think about it. A tone sounds and a message appears in the corner of my screen that tells me, "You have mail."

The problem is that I would always stop and see what e-mail just came in. Chasing rabbits. When I turned that e-mail off and only paid attention to sending and receiving e-mail at the specific times I set aside for that purpose, I was amazed at how much more I was getting done.

Do you have any examples of chasing technology rabbits in your work and life?

"Many persons have a wrong idea of what constitutes true happiness. It's not attained through self edification but through fidelity to a worthy purpose"
—Helen Keller

Rocks, Pebbles, and Sand

—Leaders know what the returns on their investments of time will be

When Mitch Huhem speaks, I listen. He had several million-dollar income streams while still only in his 20's! (www.netmarketingalliance.net)

He turned me on to this analogy: Think of a pail or bucket. Put as many rocks in the pail as you can. Now, place in as many pebbles as will fall in around the rocks. Now, pour in as much sand as will fill in around the pebbles.

Think what would happen if you did this in reverse? You start out with sand, then put a few pebbles on top, and then there wouldn't be any room for rocks.

That's one of the best time management illustrations I've seen. The rocks are what you absolutely have to get done this week. If you don't do a rock in your business or family life, things will fall apart. A rock is critical. A rock has the greatest return on investment.

Pick two rocks in different areas of your life: career, spirituality, relationships, your health, and community. Block those items on your calendar.

Now, decide what the other things you need to do, but it's not the end of the world if they don't happen. Those are the pebbles. Put those in your calendar as well.

Everything else is sand. Let the sand fill in only around what you have already blocked out.

Leaders constantly decide what the rocks in their life are for each day, week, month, year, and for their entire life.

Doing this will keep you on purpose and proactive, rather than reactive and doing the urgent but not important items. *Not everything that is good to do is the right thing for you to do.*

Average people have it backwards. (Like they do with most things in life.) They allow the sand to come in, hustle to put in a few pebbles, and have no room left for the rocks.

This is best to do on the same day, consistently every week. Many people find Sunday night a good time to do their Rocks, Pebbles, and Sand.

Whatever day of the week this day is for you, take one hour and identify two rocks in each of the major areas of your life for the next week and put them on your calendar.

Then, identify several pebbles in each of those areas for the next seven days of your life. Now, you're good to go. You know what the returns on your investments will be.

TAKEAWAY!

Not everything has the same pay off or return on investment for your time. Prioritize the things you have to do in three levels:
- Rocks—the essentials
- Pebbles—things that need to be done
- Sand—the everyday things

Action Step #1

Identify the major areas of your life, such as: career, relationship, health, community, fitness, spirituality, and fun.

List two rocks this week on your calendar for each area. These are the biggest return items that you absolutely want to get done even if you forget everything else. Now, get someone else's point of view about whether these items are really the rocks.

Action Step #2

Get a pail or bucket, some big rocks, some smaller rocks or pebbles, and some sand. Put this somewhere where you will see it daily as a trigger device.

An Example

About 100 years ago, Charles Schwab, the famous president of Bethlehem Steel, wanted to increase his personal efficiency and efficiency of the key people in his company. Ivy Lee, a highly respected "efficiency expert" approached Schwab and said, "I can increase your people's efficiency— and your sales—if you will allow me to spend just 15 minutes with each one of your executives."

Mr. Schwab asked how much that would cost, and Lee told him, "Nothing, unless it works. After three months, you can send me a check for whatever you feel it's worth to you."

That was an offer Schwab could not refuse. The next day, Lee met with Schwab's top executives. He spent just 15 minutes with each man and said the exact same thing every time.

He asked them to promise him that for the next 90 days, each evening before they left their offices, they would make a list of the six most important things they had to do the next day and number them in order of their importance. Lee told each man to scratch the item off his list when he finished and if he didn't get it done that day, move it on to the next day's list.

That was all he said. After he spoke with the last man, he left the offices of Bethlehem Steel and did not return again.

Three months later, Schwab looked over the results and was so impressed, he sent Lee a check for $35,000!

Back then the average American worker was paid $2 per day! Schwab valued Ivy Lee's contribution to his efficiency 17,500 times that for just a few hours.

> "It is only after living a fair portion of one's life that one really knows what are the things that matter, the things that will remain unto the end."
> —Esther Meynell

Be an ACTION Fanatic

—Leaders take action even when they don't know the best thing to do

Imagine five birds are sitting on a limb of a tree. Count them: one, two, three, four, and five. Three of the birds decide to fly off. How many birds are left sitting on the limb?

You might be tempted to say two, figuring five minus three equals two (5-3 = 2).

I beg to differ. I suggest all five birds are still sitting on the limb, because the decision to fly off is very different than the action of flying off! *Making a decision and actually taking action are vastly different!* Leaders take action even when they don't know the best thing to do.

We all know people who have made New Year's resolutions or decisions to do something, but have failed to take the actions necessary to make it a reality.

Go ahead and use this story with those around you. They can tell you they made a decision, but if they haven't taken the action, then they're still sitting on the limb.

Maybe someone in your business made the decision to communicate or delegate more, but if they aren't taking the actions necessary to be successful, they are still sitting on the limb.

Or maybe you have decided to lose weight or invest money, but are still thinking about what to do. Action is the key. Be an action fanatic today!

Many times the act of taking action clears the way for the proper action to be taken. When you first put yourself in motion, it may not be the best action, but it can create a better action, and another better action, and another when before you didn't know what to do.

Write down two actions that support a decision you have made recently but have been holding back on taking action. Tell them to a friend and commit to doing them this week.

TAKEAWAY!

There is a big difference between making a decision and taking action. Be an action fanatic!

Action Step #1

Make a list of five decisions you have made, such as: to lose weight, exercise, make more money, have a better relationship, invest or save money, spend more time with the children, etc. Assign each decision a specific day. Don't go to sleep each day until you have taken action on that decision.

Action Step #2

Clip out a picture or make one up of three birds flying and put it somewhere where you will see it constantly. Let this remind you that you are a person of action and that birds are actually flying off your branch.

An Example

Many years ago I was in a Shaky's pizza parlor watching a Mohammed Ali boxing match. I believe, in terms of boxing, Ali truly was the greatest.

There were about 200 people in the restaurant watching the fight on a large screen. Mohammed Ali was fighting a white boxer.

There was one guy watching who was drunk to the point of saliva dripping down his chin. He was also about six foot five and weighed around 250 pounds.

Every time the white boxer would punch Mohammed Ali, the drunk would say "stick that . . . ," using the infamous "N" word. I knew it was wrong, but didn't know what to do. My mind was telling me that if I talked to the drunk, not only might I get beat up, but he wouldn't hear or understand me anyway.

Finally, I couldn't stand it, so I walked over intending to tell him to stop using that word, but what came out of my mouth was a complete surprise to me. I said, "It's okay. I love you and it will be OK." And as I spoke, I lightly touched his shoulder.

He shoved me away and mumbled if I touched him again he would punch my lights out (or words to that affect).

I said again, "It's okay. I love you and it's going to be all right." He shoved me away and mumbled a few more things I couldn't understand. So, I sheepishly went back to my chair feeling like a failure.

Interestingly enough, within three or four minutes he left the pizza parlor. There could have been a lot of reasons he left the restaurant, but it didn't matter. The key is that the problem got solved. The action of my feet crossing the room led to a different action than I thought I was taking and the problem got solved.

> "Nobody made a greater mistake than they who did nothing because they could do only a little"
> —Edmund burke

Stretch Your Frying Pan
—Leaders have a large abundant consciousness

Imagine a man fishing. He has a bucket and a 12-inch ruler that is broken off at the 10-inch mark. He pulls in a fish and measures it. It's very small, only 7 inches, and he puts it in his bucket.

That's right! What a shocker. He keeps the little fish. Then he reels in a 24-inch whopper. Seeing it's bigger than his ruler, he throws it back in the water!

Repeatedly, the man keeps every fish smaller than 10 inches and throws all the bigger fish back.

Now, I'm not a very good fisherman, but I confront him with why he's doing this. The man tells me matter-of-factly, "My wife only has a 10-inch frying pan."

Silly story, but how often do we reject ideas as being unrealistic simply because they are bigger than our frying pan, bigger than our consciousness?

Perhaps someone has approached you with a way to make a large amount of money and you immediately reject it because it's bigger than your frying pan.

Perhaps someone has suggested you can get a project done in half the time you are thinking is possible. Did you reject it off hand as unrealistic?

Are you ready to double the size of your frying pan this year? Hanging out with people who are more successful than you is one way you can stretch your frying pan. Don't argue with them about how they are being unrealistic. Stretch your thinking.

One of the reasons I hang out with Mark Victor Hansen and Robert Allen is that my frying pan is stretched by those men!

I pre-sold 1,000 copies of my book, *If How To's Were Enough, We Would All Be Skinny Rich and Happy*. That covered my printing costs and I thought I was doing pretty well.

But Mark, who has sold over 100 million books, which makes me a novice at selling books, and Robert worked to pre-sell one million copies of *The One Minute Millionaire* before it was printed! That definitely altered my frying pan!

I recommend you purchase a frying pan and put in where you will see it a lot. Have this trigger you to keep getting a bigger and bigger frying pan.

So many people when they go to set their goals look at what they did last year and add 10 percent to that for the current year. They look as that as reasonable. It may be reasonable, but it does not generate the creative tension necessary to create enormous success.

If you want to protect yourself, then write a worst case for you to plan on. Corporately, we call that our accounting case. Then decide on a target that is much bigger than you know how to do now. That forces you to ask for help from other people and from God.

Write down two things you have said no to because you didn't think you had the time or money to do. Spend 30 minutes this week thinking about those two things and the question, "If I really had to, how would I do that?"

That will stretch your frying pan.

TAKEAWAY!

The size of the frying pan determines the size of the fish you can catch and keep. Leaders have a large abundant consciousness.

Action Step #1

Have lunch with someone that is way more successful than you. Interview them. Look for what they're doing that to you would be "unrealistic." Ask them what makes that so realistic for them.

Action Step #2

Identify your limits. What is the maximum increase in financial income you can conceive happening to you this year? What is the quickest amount of time you can make a true friend? What is the largest amount of money you can raise and contribute to a community organization?

An Example

Often in our Personal Mastery Seminars I will take someone that has a migraine headache and do a technique with them that in less than five minutes—with no drugs—eliminates the headache. It's available on one of the CD's in our Pursuit and Practice of Personal Mastery series.

Part of the reason I do the technique, is because it's good for people to have a tool to handle headaches that can augment and often replace drugs. I did this just recently in the hair saloon where I get my hair cut with another patron. It shocked them so much they cried on my shoulder.

The biggest reason I do it, is because it shatters people's frying pan's of what is possible. When someone actually gets rid of a migraine in less than five minutes, when they normally would have to take shots or go home, they begin to doubt their self-imposed limits. They start to wonder about other things, such as turning a marriage around or perhaps living a lifestyle they thought was just an impossible dream.

> "The only place where your dream becomes impossible is in your own thinking"
> —Robert Schuller

Prices vs. Benefits

—Leaders have a great awareness of the benefits and prices of their choices

In our teen leadership classes, the theme is every moment is a choice and every choice has both benefits and prices to be paid. Both parts are usually difficult for the teens to grasp.

They will argue that they have to go to school. We tell them it is a choice and they don't have to go. They argue for a while and then one of them usually says something like, "If we don't go to school, they will put us in jail." Our facilitator agrees. Yes, they will put you in some kind of juvenile delinquent center. That's called a consequence. It is a price to be paid.

The teenagers begin to see that they have lots of choices and they choose based on the perceived consequences, positive and negative.

Then we take them into exploring hidden consequences. What if you touched a stove but due to a time delay or many things happening at once you never understood it was the stove that was burning you? You would touch the stove a lot more than would be good for you.

Many times the prices are hidden. Part of the problem is that prices hurt, so we don't even want to look at them. Suppose a manager shows up for a meeting five minutes late. In most people's mind the price paid was the lost five minutes of information. Maybe the meeting wasn't even going to start on time, so possibly there is no price paid.

The hidden prices are very high, but not seen. For example, the manager's word has no value now. Later, suppose he says to himself, "I will lose 15 pounds." His sub-conscious immediately speaks up, "Who are you trying to kid. You couldn't even keep that time agreement for the meeting. You will never lose the weight."

Having your word lose all its power is a huge price!

Or, suppose others in the group begin to not trust the manager. They don't take risks in their work and perhaps the project doesn't succeed because of that. That's a huge price.

Leaders look at every moment as a choice and have a great awareness of the benefits and prices of that choice. Be a leader and look for the hidden prices.

There are benefits also. Sometimes we think that because of bad behavior or where we are victim of circumstance that there are no benefits. That is not true. That is why you do what you do even when the outcome is not what you want.

Victims, for example, hate the circumstance, but they do get lots of attention and they don't have to change. They sometimes even get control over other people.

But what about the prices? *This is important because no one changes anything until they see the prices are higher than they want to pay.*

TAKEAWAY!

Look for the hidden prices that are even more expensive than those that are obvious. These are the behavior changers.

Action Step #1

Look back over the last five years of your life and pick one or two major choices you've made. What were the benefits and prices (and hidden prices) of those choices?

Action Step #2

Make a list this week of the prices you are paying and the benefits you are getting for living your life right now.

An Example

I enjoy playing golf, although I don't make the time to play often. Golf is a great teacher. I read this piece a number of years ago about an up-and-coming golfer named Billy Ray Brown. It was titled, "Paying the price for one bad shot." Here's the story:

The wrist was in good hands. A doctor and a couple of trainers had already bent and manipulated the joint, finding no broken bones and no major damage.

They'd pulled out the ice pack and were going through the litany of things for Tiger Woods to do in the next 36 hours. Woods' coach, Butch Harmon, was shaking his head, having delivered the what-in-the-heck-were-you-thinking speech after watching Woods take out a rock—instead of taking a drop—to hit a shot.

The door to the fitness trailer opened and Billy Ray Brown blew in. He'd seen the shot and, as soon as the tour Championship telecast signed off, he headed straight for Woods. Brown pulled the splint off his right wrist and shoved it in Woods' face.

"Look pal," he said, pointing to the not-yet-healed stitches from an experimental surgery. "It's not a shot. It's a career." The ugly scar, and Brown, got Woods' attention. "Listen to me," Brown said. "It could cost you."

One shot on the third hole at Colonial Country Club. One tree root. One swing. Seven years later, Brown's right wrist is a shadow of its former self and he's still struggling to find the game that once had so much promise.

Leaders have a great awareness of the benefits and prices of their choices.

"If physical death is the price that I must pay to free my white brothers and sisters from a permanent death of spirit, then nothing can be more redemptive"
—Martin Luther King Jr.

To Push or Not to Push? That is the Question.

—Leaders push themselves when they are winning and take the pressure off when things are not going right

Years ago, my mentor took me to the horse races at Del Mar Raceway in California. He said that this was an awareness test and asked me to watch the first race and tell him what I saw. I told him I saw a bunch of four legged animals running around in circles. Wrong answer.

He instructed me to watch the second race and tell him what I saw. I told him I saw a bunch of foolish people in the stands throwing their money away betting. "Not the answer I am looking for," he replied.

This went on for three more races. Finally he said, "In the next race, watch which horses they are whipping."

In the next race I saw that only the horses in the front half of the pack were whipped. He told me to remember that.

Most people have it backwards. When you are doing well, that's when you want to whip yourself to go faster. But most people, if they do well, reward themselves by taking the afternoon or week off.

In the military there is an interesting principle where you reinforce when you are winning. If you break through an enemy's position, that is when you send in reserves to deepen the penetration of your force.

When you are doing poorly, like the horses coming in last, don't whip yourself. Take the afternoon off. That's when most people whip themselves to work harder—when they aren't doing so well.

They have it backwards.

When you are not doing well, take time off, get your head straight and then tackle the business at hand or whatever the project is. Most people have it backwards and whip themselves at the wrong time.

TAKEAWAY!

When you are doing well, push yourself harder. When you are doing poorly, take time off to get your attitude straight.

Action Step #1

Take a moment to think of where in your life you are pushing yourself hard and getting little return. Are you working even more hours at work and making little or no more money?

Are you spending more time in a relationship but it is not getting more intimate or exciting? Are you praying exhaustively and not getting more intimate with God?

Now, find a way to take a break so that when you go back to that activity it is with a different viewpoint.

Action Step #2

Take a moment to identify where you have momentum in your success. How can you push yourself even more in that area?

An Example

When my mentor took me to the horse races, I was a marketing director for his seminars in San

Diego, California. I had had tremendous success building the attendance up from nine people in a seminar when I got there to 70 people! Then things started to slide.

I pressed myself harder to try and turn it around. The marketing plan involved many volunteers. As I pressed myself harder I became less fun or inspirational to be around so fewer volunteers helped. So, I pressed myself even harder and fewer volunteers came around.

The downward spiral had sunk to where we had only 32 people in a class. That was when my mentor stepped in to correct the belief systems that were running my behavior.

He had me take a week off in Mexico, and when I came back I was totally refreshed and the class size started to increase—even though there was one week less to build the seminar, because of my vacation.

"Associate yourself with men of good quality if you esteem your own reputation. It is better to be alone than in bad company"
—George Wahington

Don't Let Them Pull You Back
—Leaders are not victim to what others think

Years ago, a man by the name of Conrad Salas, who was raised in the deserts of New Mexico, was visiting Galveston, Texas. As he passed through a fish market, he saw a shallow pan of crabs outside a shopkeeper's store.

Conrad went inside and warned the shopkeeper he better get a deeper pan or the crabs would get away. The shopkeeper told him not to worry about it, explaining that whenever one crab tried to crawl out, the others would always drag it back into the pan.

Although any crab could easily have gotten out of the pan by itself, none ever did. Conrad thought that pretty much summed up his life.

From his viewpoint, he had been brought up on the wrong side of the tracks. Every time he tried to change, someone would try and pull him back saying something like, "Who do you think you are?" or "We liked the old you better."

You too, will face such crabs. Every time you risk, there will be someone trying to prevent you from changing. Many times, it is from those who care about you the most. It's not that they don't love you. It's that they are afraid of losing you by being left behind.

You will be faced with the decision of allowing yourself to be pulled back in the pan or continuing to crawl out.

Obviously, I support you on continuing to change and crawling out. The good news to that option is that, usually, you pull a few crabs out of the pan with you.

Take 15 minutes right now and take an inventory of the people you hang out with. Are they pulling you back into the status quo or encouraging you to take risks and move forward?

It doesn't mean you have to cut them out of your life, but you may want to move certain people from your inner circle to a more outer circle of influence in your life and spend less time with them.

Everyone has support groups, but we need to ask ourselves what they are supporting us in doing. Sometimes we have friends supporting us in drinking a lot or being lazy or in listening to negative talk.

TAKEAWAY!

There are people, places, and things that pull us back from our growth to keep us comfortable. Others don't want you to change, not because they don't love you, but because they are afraid for you or for themselves.

Action Step #1

Pick one person who is a friend you spend a large amount of time with that does not support you in changing. Pick someone who lives at a higher level than you in terms of relationships, financially, spiritually, or the difference they make in the community.

Consciously reduce the time you spend with the former and increase the time you spend with the latter. It's just like breaking a habit. It's easier to replace a habit with another, better one, than to simply try to get rid of a bad one.

Action Step #2

Look around you in your professional life. Do you have people that are stuck in the old way of doing things? Look at your spiritual life. Do you have people that do not support your growth, because it scares them or threatens their power in the bureaucracy of the organization?

Do you have friends who don't want you to leave for better opportunities? Find a group or form a mastermind that will support you in your growth regardless of the consequences to them.

An Example

My wife had a friend from her early adulthood who always overspent her personal budget. Whenever they went out together, she would encourage my wife to buy things.

Roma, my wife, would get home and look at the things she bought that she really didn't want or need and feel bad.

Whenever my wife would try and bring the subject up to her friend, the other woman would get very defensive.

This friend had been a convenient friend because she was single and when I was traveling on business trips it was more awkward for my wife to mix with couples when she was alone.

Finally, my wife decided that she had to reduce the amount of time she spent with this other woman. It was uncomfortable for my wife to make new friends, but that is what she did so that she didn't have the negative pull any longer.

I experienced a similar thing in my business as we grew. In the early days, everyone had plenty of my attention, because we were few in number. As we grew larger I had to delegate and couldn't be everywhere.

Some of my leaders didn't want us to grow simply so they could have all of my attention.

We discussed the situation so they were clear that less of my time did not mean I didn't care for them as much.

This reduced some of their fear and some of them changed because they were committed to our growth, and some ended up leaving.

I kept focused on the growth.

> "Great spirits have always encountered violent opposition from mediocre minds"
> —Albert Einstein

Living Up or Down?

—Leaders give themselves and others a reputation to live up to, not one equal to their track record that is reasonable

In 1952, a fifth grade teacher told her students about a study that conclusively proved that people with brown eyes were not as smart as those with blue eyes. She then proceeded to put collars on the brown-eyed students.

That day all kinds of things happened, one of which was that the brown-eyed student's test scores immediately dropped significantly and the blue-eyed students test scores soared.

The next day she told her students that she had made a mistake reading the information and that it was actually the blue-eyed students that were slower mentally and poorer performers.

They switched the collars over to the blue-eyed students and that same day the blue-eyed student's test scores dropped significantly and the brown-eyed students scores soared.

One of the many things that came out of this study is that *people live up to or down to the reputation they are being given*.

What kind of reputation are you giving your spouse? Is it one to live up to? Is it one to live down to? Is it one equal to his or her track record?

Your potential has no correlation to your track record. All a track record shows is what belief systems you have been operating from in the past. Since these belief systems are not fixed and can be changed, there is no relationship between your past and your potential.

If you have business partners, what kind of reputation are you giving them? Is it a reputation equal to their track record with you? One to live down to? Or one to live up to?

Perhaps most importantly, what kind of reputation are you giving yourself? Is it a reputation equal to your track record? Or is it one to live up to?

Focus this week on giving yourself a reputation to live up to and doing the same for others.

TAKEAWAY!

We live up or down to the reputation we are given. Many people use their past as the reputation or the expectation they go by. This is being victim to the past. Anyone's past is only a measure of the belief systems that have made their decisions, NOT their true capabilities.

Action Step #1

List one reputation you have been giving yourself that is equal to your past. Now, consciously choose an expectation or reputation for you to live up to in that area. Find someone else who has made that kind of change to give yourself hope and encouragement.

Action Step #2

Identify a child, boss, or employee who you have been holding less than capable because of their past. Now, let go of that and choose a new expectation or reputation for that person to live up to.

An Example

In the mid seventies when I was first working for my mentor Tom, he sent me on an assignment that had nothing to do with my previous work experience. I had been learning how to facilitate his seminars and previous to that had been an infantry officer.

Tom sent me from San Francisco to Eugene, Oregon on two hours notice to turn a marketing area around that most executives in the company thought we should shut down permanently, Tom had belief that I could do it.

It took me twice as long to solve the problem as he envisioned, but I solved it. I had no marketing experience and no experience handling confrontational situations where an employee was basically trying to steal part of the company.

Tom simply believed in me and held an expectation that I could solve the problem. Even though I had my struggles, that totally changed my belief in myself as well as how I was held in everyone else's eyes in the company.

Leaders must not be afraid to put their people in tough situations and hold them capable of solving the problem. That is how you develop true leaders in your organization.

"I have no right by anything I say or do to demean a human being in his own eyes. What matters is not what I think of him. It is what he thinks of himself. To undermine a man's self respect is a sin."
—Antoine de Saint-Exupery

Failing Forward

—Leaders detest failure, but embrace it without fearing it

Several weeks after I went to work for my mentor Tom, he asked how I was doing. I told him I was doing great. I loved working for him. Then he asked me if I had made a big mistake somewhere on my job?

I got worried and thought over all the tasks I had done. After reflection, I proudly replied, "No, I haven't made any big mistakes."

Then Tom said, "Oh. Then we have a serious problem. I've fired people for a lack of integrity and I have fired them for not taking risks, but I have never fired someone for making a mistake. You have two weeks to go make a big mistake."

I was flabbergasted. I'd never worked for someone like this before. Most of my army career I tried not to make any mistakes, and if I made some, I tried to cover them up so no one would know.

He was not asking me to purposely fail. He was asking me to keep taking risks until I didn't succeed. Tom was beginning the process of my learning to be "flat on failure."

So many people have such a huge attachment to failure they are avoiding failure rather than pursuing success. That's playing life with a "not to lose" strategy instead of a "maximum gain strategy."

If you want to up your success level, then up your failure rate. Make a list of what risks you are avoiding in your business life. Then make a list of what risks you are avoiding in your personal life. Now, commit to taking risks until you don't succeed.

If you were told to climb a tall fruit tree and pick the fruit out on the limbs, the natural tendency would be to hold on to the tree truck with one hand and reach for the fruit with the other. The goal somehow becomes, "do not fall" instead of "get out on the limbs and gather the fruit." Fear of falling tries to override the desire and potential for gain.

TAKEAWAY!

To increase your success, increase the size of your failures.

Action Step #1

List your biggest failure in the past year. Commit to taking risks in that area until you make a bigger failure.

Action Step #2

People will take bigger risks when there is a safety net. What can you do to build a safety net for your self-esteem so that it does not suffer when you have a "failure"?

An Example

In Frank Betger's classic book, *How I raised myself from failure to success in selling*, he talks about embracing failure in prospecting.

In the beginning, he avoided prospecting new customers to avoid failing. It was obvious that wasn't going to work. He found out that it took the average person 19 prospecting calls before they made a sale.

So, he put 19 pennies in his right pocket. After each prospecting call he moved one penny from the right pocket to the left pocket. That way, instead of fearing a "no," he just focused on moving pennies from one pocket to the other.

He was embracing failure, but putting no energy on it. Failing or getting a "no" didn't mean he was no good as a salesman, it just meant he was closer to a "yes." It might be the first call or it might be the 19th, but he knew he would make the sale eventually.

"One must be a god to be able to tell success from failures without making a mistake"
—Anton Chekhov

Following the Leader
—Good leaders must first be good followers

There is an animal called a lemming. It's famous for jumping off cliffs and committing suicide by the thousands. One lemming simply follows another who follows another, on and on to their death. Sadly, most people are like that.

Show me someone in an organization who talks badly about other people or talks negative about "the company" and I will show you a whole bunch of people who negatively gossip. They are not bad people, they are just "lemmings."

Show me a student who uses illegal drugs and I will show you a whole bunch of other students who use illegal drugs. They are "lemmings."

Now, the principle also works in reverse. Show me one employee who calls on another employee and says, "Excuse me. We don't speak negatively about people behind their back here. If you have a problem, talk to them directly. There's a phone. Call them now and I'll watch." When you have that, not too many people will be negatively gossiping around you.

Again, it is not because they are good people. They just lucked out in the direction of the head lemming.

This is not to say, "Following is bad." I attended West Point, the United States Military Academy. One of our first lessons was, "To be a good leader, you must first be a good follower."

If you are not willing to follow someone or something, then why would anyone follow you? They wouldn't! You do want to follow so you can generate that in others.

The question becomes: "What or who are you following and why?"

Do you have a set of principles you have examined and have consciously committed yourself to? If so, that will empower you as a leader. If you haven't, then you will be a lemming.

Is following an addiction where you cannot lead? If so, then you will be a lemming. List one person you are willing to follow. List two principles you are willing to follow.

TAKEAWAY!

There is nothing wrong with following the crowd if it is going your way. If you are only following the crowd to fit in, you will pay a heavier price than you realize or want.

Action Step #1

List one person you have been unwilling to follow, simply because you resist authority.

Action Step# 2

List a person or principle you are willing to follow. List three actions that are uncomfortable, but you will take action on this week that demonstrate you are following.

An Example

As I mentioned, I am a graduate of West Point. The very first thing they have you do when you report your first day is to drop the travel bags you are carrying. They then tell you that you hadn't done it fast enough and have you pick them up and do it again.

We must have dropped the bags half a dozen times before they told us anything else. It was the beginning of learning to follow.

There were many times later on where that would come to have value. You would be placed in a situation and told to do something that you might not agree with or that was difficult (not immoral, just a different viewpoint), but we had been trained to follow authority, so we were able to. It was learning to follow the right authority.

There was a rule at the academy that you could not be married. One of my best friends at the academy got a lady pregnant and left the academy so he could marry her. He followed his principles—a good thing. He is still married today 32 years later.

Many cadets got married the first week after graduation. It was almost a "thing."

I was in love and didn't want to follow the crowd, simply because I was rebellious, so I didn't propose or get married just to not follow the crowd. That ended the relationship.

So, it is important to be OK with following, not being ruled by independence or rebelliousness, but it is important to know and choose the right thing person or principles to follow.

"To command is to serve, nothing more and nothing less."
—Andre Malraux

Leaders Know WHY

—Leaders know it is more important to know the why than the how

My mentor taught me that he who knows why will always employ he who knows how. Those who just know how work for others.

Most people just want to know what they are supposed to do or say. A person beginning in sales, for example, will often want to know what they are supposed to say to get someone interested in their product or service.

That's OK, but it is limited. With a different type of prospect you have to say the exact same thing because all you have is your script. You want to learn why are you saying this first and why do you tell this or that story.

That way, you know what to change and what not to change in different situations or with different prospects. Corporations spend thousands of dollars working on their mission statement. What are we really all about?

If you don't know why you are in business, you can create lots of "sacred cow" things you do because you have always done them that way and yet with changes in technology they are no longer applicable.

People spend years developing how to earn a living, but sometimes don't even spend a week determining why they are even alive. What is the point of your existence? Isn't that a good question? Don't back off from it. It can be scary to think about, but it pays huge dividends when you know the answer.

This not only guides decision making as to "what" to do but gives you the passion or fuel to grind it out during those discouraging times.

Make a list of the reasons why you work where you work (a friend recommended you, you grew up near there, etc.) Then ask yourself: Does this job fit why you exist (your purpose).

Work is meant to be an expression of your purpose. If it doesn't match up or is not the best match up, don't panic. It does not mean you must change jobs instantly. At least you have your eyes open for opportunities that are more in alignment with your purpose.

TAKEAWAY!

It is more important to know the "why" than the "how." He who knows why will always employ he who knows how.

Action Step #1

At the end of one day this week, write down what you did during the day: phone calls made, projects worked on, etc.

Action Step #2

Then, write down why you did each one. Which ones were consciously chosen and which ones were based out of habit, convenience, or a reaction?

An Example

When I train facilitators for our seminars, their first assignment is to take a pad of paper and draw a vertical line down the center.

On the left hand side they write "**What**." On the right hand side they write "**Why**."

As they watch a seminar being done they will write on the left hand side all the "whats" they see. These might include how the chairs were set up, a story I told, how I was dressed, etc.

Then they have to figure out why I had the chairs like that, why did I tell that story and why did I tell it when I did.

The course content I can teach in a relatively short period of time, but if you don't know all the "whys," then you are stuck to a certain script. If circumstances change—like the seminar is 10 times as big or the group is much older or more skeptical—and you only know the what or how, then you can only do that same script and it probably won't work.

If you know why you are doing everything, then you can change "what" you are doing in a new circumstance to fulfill the "why."

You are much more effective. You are a better leader.

"He who knows why will always employ
he who knows how"
—Thomas Willhite

The Zen of Leadership

—Leaders know how to be focused and relaxed at the same time

Focus is a fundamental skill of anyone who has mastered anything, whether it is music, race car driving, being an engineer, parenting, or sales.

It is one of our "10 traits of a Compassionate Samurai." A compassionate samurai is someone who is a bold, ethical leader whose life is devoted to being of service.

We have several experiential exercises people do to get better at being focused and relaxed at the same time in our Personal Mastery and Advanced Leadership seminars.

Average people, if they are very focused, get up tight. If they are very relaxed, they get unfocused. The key is to be both at the same time.

Think of a conflict situation. Average people, if they step in to help resolve the conflict, get caught up in the emotion and are up tight. The key is to be calm in the midst of conflict if you are to resolve it.

Give someone the responsibility of a big job, such as raising all the money needed for a new school, and they become focused and uptight. Ask someone to simply be a worker on the school committee and they're relaxed.

Average people have no real mental discipline. If you put them in an extreme situation, such as financial problems, all they can think about are the financial problems. They are mentally undisciplined.

Leaders are able to discipline themselves to think about solutions, even when they are knee deep in problems.

Practice concentrating on what you want to focus on, rather than allow your mind to drift or be distracted by circumstances around you.

Once a day for a week, focus on one item, such as a ballpoint pen, for just five minutes. Become aware of when and how often your mind drifts away.

Constantly bringing your focus back to the pen is like increasing the strength of your muscles by lifting weights. Your ability to focus on what you want will only increase with proper training.

TAKEAWAY!

Be relaxed and focused at the same time. Focusing is a fundamental skill and is required to become a master of anything.

Action Step #1

Practice being relaxed right now.

Action Step #2

Then practice being relaxed in what is a normally tense situation, such as a job interview or having an uncomfortable conversation with a child or spouse.

One way to practice being relaxed is simply to visualize a relaxing nature scene, such as your garden or being on the beach. Your body responds to mental images, not reality. If you ever had a nightmare, you know your body responded to the mental alligators chasing you, not the comfortable warm bed you were in.

Tenseness is a result of your subconscious seeing a picture of an unfavorable outcome. If you are disciplined, you can choose a picture that has the reverse effect, calms you down and has you focus.

An Example

In the late '70s, my mentor had 40 men out at his ranch. I was one of them. He asked us all to pull 100 dollars out of our pockets. Some didn't have that much cash on them and others were afraid of what he was going to do.

He then held up a rifle and gave everyone five bullets. He said we would go one at a time shooting at individual targets and we would have one minute to get all five shots off. Best score won all the money.

The first person to go raised the rifle and just as he was about to shoot, my mentor unexpectedly screamed in his ear! The person shot wildly off the target, because he jerked the gun up. Then he froze, not understanding what had just happened.

Tom started laughing and told him he might as well put the gun down, because he now only had four shots and had wasted 15 seconds. The gentlemen put the gun down and walked away.

This same thing continued with all 40 of us— Tom, always screaming in the shooters ear. You better believe we ALL screamed in his ear when it was his turn. He still won. I came in second.

Afterwards, he explained how this imitated life. The potential to lose 100 dollars or win 4000 dollars simulated the money pressures of life. The one-minute time limit simulated the time pressures of life. The screaming simulated the distractions we all experience in raising children, doing our work or

Leading an organization.

In shooting a rifle, you must be relaxed, because tension destroys your accuracy. You must also be focused or you miss the target.

It's a lesson I have never forgotten. Well worth my 100 dollars!

"When you are doing your best work it will seem effortless."
—Bill Diffenderfer

Birds of a Feather
—Leaders know who to associate with and why

Leaders consciously cultivate relationships with very successful people. Aristotle Onasis once said that if he lost all his money he could recreate the wealth. To do that, the most important thing he would do is get in the presence of wealthy people.

He then explained why that is so very important. There were three reasons:

#1) Wealthy people knew experts that could help you out with any project.

#2) Wealthy people had money to finance your good ideas.

#3) Wealthy people had good ideas they didn't have time to follow through on and that you could.

I will add one more reason.

#4) By observing wealthy people, you can learn how they think.

Make it your mission this week to spend time around a very wealthy person. This may take some work. You may not live, work, or play around very wealthy people. If you are to catch a moose, you must go to where the moose are. You can be the best moose hunter in the world, but if you are looking for one in the downtown shopping mall, you will come away empty handed.

Do your homework and find out what restaurants they frequent? Where do wealthy people work out? What church of your faith has attracted wealthy people? Can you get tickets through a friend or even a scalper for luxury box seats to a sports event you like? What conferences do wealthy people attend?

You must increase your courage and actually talk with the people you are intimidated by. Why would they want to spend time with you? What can you do for them? How can you be of service to them?

Make your conversation about them and develop a relationship with them. If you are successful, there will be plenty of other opportunities to ask them for knowledge, contacts, etc.

TAKEAWAY!

Spend time and money cultivating influential friends. Wealthy people have expert contacts, money to invest in your ideas, new ideas they will give you to follow up on, and they can teach you through their actions how to think "wealthy".

Action Step #1

Ask the pastor of your church or the head of a service organization (such as Rotary) who are the three wealthiest people in their organization. Let that person know you are doing interviews, like Napoleon Hill did to create the classic *Think & Grow Rich.*

Call the people you are referred to and ask to take them to lunch at the nicest place in town for a one-hour interview. Question them on tips they would want their children to know about accumulating wealth, managing wealth, and investing wealth to make a difference. Find out where they play, go to church, what clubs they are a part of, seminars they attend, what charities they support.

Make a list of questions you want answers to including what are their current challenges. Listen from a place of how you might be of service. Make sure you ask how you can be of service to them. Become a friend looking for how you might give to them, instead of just what you are learning from them.

Action Step #2

Find a charity you believe in that attracts wealthy people. Volunteer to help on some committee alongside them.

An Example

For the last eleven years, I have attended Bob Harrison's Hawaii increase event. Bob is a great teacher who is known world wide as "Dr. Increase". His event is held every spring at a resort on one of the Islands of Hawaii. His main theme is "increase." They even call him "Dr. Increase." It's a great place for me to get renewed spiritually.

One of the reasons I go to his events is the wonderful achievers that I meet and the fellowship we enjoy. It is also a great place for me to get renewed physically and spiritually.

The tuition for the seminar itself is relatively inexpensive, (less than $1000 for a family for the whole week). The event attracts higher-achievers and successful business people there. Since the seminar sessions are held during the mornings there's plenty of time to get to know people and enjoy the island paradise.

One year, I had a graduate of our seminars there who is a good friend now, Steve St. Martin. He was just moving into real estate development. At the conference was the number one developer in the state of Washington. I introduced them to each other.

They didn't do business together, but the sharing of ideas caused Steve to get a million dollar signature loan for one of his projects.

Another example of choosing friends happened in 1981, when I lived in San Diego. I interviewed several Toastmaster clubs looking to see which one to join. One of them was called "Professional Men's 624."

Now, most clubs just charge for the breakfast or dessert when you show up. I liked Professional Men's 624, because they charged for all the meals for the whole calendar quarter up front. You didn't spend any more money then if you attended regularly, but you would be surprised how it weeded out people with "poverty of the brainstem." That club had attracted some of the most successful business people in town at that time.

"The key is to keep company only with people that uplift you, whose presence calls forth your best"
—Epictetus

If It Feels Good, Do It. NOT!

—Leaders do today what will feel good tomorrow while average people simply do what feels good today

Leaders do today what will feel good tomorrow. Average people simply do what feels good.

Back in the '60s there was a slogan among the hippies, "Hey, if it feels good, do it." That was a half-truth that got distorted. From drugs to sex, it felt good at that moment, but you sure don't feel good tomorrow. Similarly, being lazy and procrastinating on things you need to do feels good in the moment, but you don't feel good tomorrow.

Other things don't feel good today, but do feel good tomorrow. Studying for school may not feel good today, but it feels good tomorrow. Having a needed but uncomfortable conversation with someone does not feel good in the moment, but it feels good tomorrow. Making a prospecting call may not feel good today in the moment, but it feels good tomorrow. Exercise may not feel good today, but it feels good tomorrow.

So, one key my mentor taught me: do only those things that will feel good tomorrow . . . today.

TAKEAWAY!

Do today what feels good tomorrow. If it won't feel good tomorrow . . . don't do it today.

Action Step #1

Make a list of those things you are doing today that feel good today, but do not feel good tomorrow. Don't procrastinate or you will have one more thing on your list!

Action Step #2

Make a list of things that don't feel good today that you are not doing, but if you did them, you would feel good tomorrow.

An Example

One of the most inspiring poems I've ever read is "IF" by Rudyard Kipling. It is filled with examples of things that didn't feel good today, but most certainly will feel good tomorrow.

If you can keep your head when all about you Are losing theirs and blaming it on you,

If you can trust yourself when all men doubt you, But make allowance for their doubting too;

If you can wait and not be tired by waiting, Or being lied about, don't deal in lies, Or being hated don't give way to hating, And yet don't look too good, nor talk too wise;

If you can dream—and not make dreams your master;

If you can think—and not make thought your aim;

If you can meet with Triumph and Disaster And treat those two impostors just the same;

If you can bear to hear the truth you've spoken Twisted by knaves to make a trap for fools, Or watch the things you gave your life to, broken, and stoop and build 'em up with worn-out tools:

If you can make one heap of all your winnings and risk it on one turn of pitch-and-toss, And lose, and start again at your beginnings And never breathe a word about your loss; To serve your turn long after they are gone, And so hold on when there is nothing in you Except the Will which says to them: "Hold on!"

If you can talk with crowds and keep your virtue, Or walk with Kings—nor lose the common touch,

If neither foes nor loving friends can hurt you,

If all men count with you, but none too much;

If you can fill the unforgiving minute with sixty seconds' worth of distance run, Yours is the Earth and everything that's in it, And—which is more—you'll be a Man, my son!

"Let me give you one definition of ethics: It is good to maintain life and to further life; it is bad to damage and destroy life. And this ethic, profound, universal, has the significance of a religion."
—Albert Schweitzer

Promises and Requests

—Leaders use a communication tool called "Promise and Request"

Leaders communicate clearly and specifically. It is a great framework from which to communicate down the line to your team, coworkers, and family members.

Many people are vague in their communication. The "benefit" of being vague is: we don't feel as confined, we don't get as much rejection, and we usually feel more comfortable.

The problem with being vague is we don't produce as much results and we set ourselves and others up for disappointment.

Promises are simply that. You are promising to do something. When you are promising to do something, it has a clear outcome by a specific time, such as, "I promise to come home by midnight" or "I'll give you a raise when this specific performance level is met."

Requests, on the other hand, are simply asking the other person to do something specific. The other person then may agree, say "no," or renegotiate, which in turn results in a new request he/she can agree to.

Two examples of requests would be: "Son, I want you home by midnight. Do you agree to that?" and "I request you support me in achieving this specific performance level by training me for one hour each day for the first two weeks. Will you do that?"

> ## TAKEAWAY!
> Promises and requests take the vagueness out of your communication by being clear and specific.

Action Step #1

Make two lists: One titled: "Promises" and the other "Requests." Go over your communications for the past week looking for instances when you've been unclear or vague. Write down new clear and specific promises or requests for each one and communicate those to the people involved.

Action Step #2

Make at least three promises and three requests every day this week in your work or home life. Compare your results this week to what you accomplished last week and notice if there's a difference.

An Example

One great place to see promises and requests in action, or the lack of them, is watching parents and children.

Jim Fay has worked with kids and families for 47 years. During all that time, he says, he's never met a child who failed to hear a parent's promise. They always hear promises the first time, and, he adds, he's also learned their ears work the same way for requests.

Jim says, "You can train your child to hear you the first time you say something. Or, you can train them to ignore you."

Jim was in an airport and observed Joshua, a five-year-old, was running out into the concourse.

"Joshua! You stop that running!" called his mother. She did not follow through, so Joshua continued dashing in and out of a crowd of irritated travelers.

"Joshua! You get over here!" Once more, she barked an order, but did nothing to enforce it.

"Joshua! Get off of that!" Another order was shouted by mom and ignored by Joshua.

Suddenly, Joshua was right at Jim's feet staring up at him.

Mother ordered again, "Joshua. You get away from that man. You come over here. Quit bothering people."

Jim looked down at Joshua and asked, "Joshua, what's your mom going to do if you don't do what she says?"

Joshua knew the answer immediately, "Nothing."

In fact, Joshua never had to walk back to his mother in the airport. She came over to Jim, held Joshua's hand, and apologized to Jim, saying, "I'm so sorry. You know how five-year-olds are. They won't listen to a thing you say."

It took Jim a lot to keep from saying, "I've known a lot of five-year-olds who listen to their parents, but their parents mean what they say."

It's all about making Promises and Requests.

> "When all is said and done, more is said than done."
> —Lou Holtz

Accounting 101

—Leaders hold themselves and others accountable without being judgmental

Accountability is a foundational principle of leadership. It is different than responsibility, although often people use these words interchangeably—and leaders do both. Accountability is to accurately account for things.

Think of accountants. Their job is to track where money comes from and where it goes. CEOs, rather than accountants, make decisions from that data. It is the job of accountants to accurately assess where everything came from and where everything goes. Telling the truth about how we have impacted a situation requires radical honesty.

Few people actually like to be held accountable. Many times people of authority try to avoid being accountable (just like people on the bottom of the authority ladder). The higher you get in an organization, the less people you have who will hold you accountable. Your authority intimidates people.

Leaders set up people and systems to insure accountability actually takes place.

Start with a person and then add a system. An "Accountability Partner" is what best selling author Ken Blanchard (www.kenblanchard.com) calls a truth teller. It's someone you feel safe with, that you can tell anything to, so that you are very open and honest with that person. You aren't telling the whole world, just that one person.

It is also someone who is not intimidated by you and who will ask the needed, but intrusive questions and not just let you slide. This would be someone you actually report to on a regular basis about what you said you would do and what you actually did. You may set up different people for different areas of your life.

Interview a few friends this week and find out who would be suitable. Then agree on a consistent process of reviewing what you said you would do, what you did do, and what you commit to doing.

If you believe as I do that spiritually there will be a great accounting one day, then this process will be a great rehearsal. If you only get one chance, wouldn't you want to rehearse for the big day?

When was the last time you did a physical accounting? Spiritual accounting? Financial accounting? If you run a department, team, or company, start looking for systems that will support individuals in being accountable.

In our corporate seminars we always establish accountability partners and they have questions to review that will assist each other in digesting or applying and understanding the material presented.

TAKEAWAY!

Lack of an accountability partner is a telltale sign of your future demise.

Action Step #1

Interview and select someone as your truth telling accountability partner. Agree on how often you are going to meet. Monthly should be an absolute minimum.

Action Step #2

Sit with this accountability partner and do a session on financial accountability, health accountability, relationship accountability, and spiritual accountability. You can add your own areas to this such as contribution accountability, career, etc.

An Example

In a study done of 150 leaders of churches who had fallen from their position, they looked for a common denominator.

There was only thing: Not one of those former leaders had a specific person who held them accountable.

> "Choice of attention - to pay attention to this and ignore that - is to the inner life what choice of action is to the outer. In both cases, a man is responsible for his choice and must accept the consequences, whatever they may be."
> —W.H. Auden

Accentuate the Positive to Eliminate the Negative

—Leaders do not tolerate negative conversation

Imagine you are sitting in your living room. You hear a knock at the door. You open the door and it's one of your good friends. He or she is dragging a trashcan full of yucky, stinky, garbage. You say, "Hi, come on in." He comes in and proceeds to dump the gooey garbage on your nice living room rug.

You might be saying to yourself, "I would never allow him into my house carrying that garbage." **Then why do you allow people to dump all their negative conversation on you?**

Do you think to be a nice person that you are obligated to hear all of someone's garbage? NO!

And if your friend dumped his garbage on your rug, would you just scrape it up and take it to someone else? That's what happens when people dump their negative garbage on you. You pass it on by telling someone, "Do you know what so and so said?" And then there's always a stain left behind.

You do not have to accept someone's negative conversation in order to qualify as a nice person and certainly not to qualify as a leader. Leaders would interrupt and say, "I can best serve you by knowing why you are telling me this. Are you needing to be heard or are you interested in solving the problem?" That clarifies your response.

Sometimes people have had a bad day, or hour, or meeting, and they need to vent. Blowing off steam is not only an OK thing to do, it is vital. It's like becoming your own self-cleaning oven.

If you are allowing others to vent, make sure they are clear that's what they are doing. Ask yourself, "Am I the one that can resolve this?" If you cannot, then have them go tell the person who can provide the solution because you don't want to hear it or your organization does not support that kind of conversation.

You can say, "In fact, there is a phone, call him or her right now and I will support you."

Another simple thing to do when you are around a negative person: do all the talking. That will insure the conversation stays positive.

TAKEAWAY!
Leaders do not allow those around them to talk negatively. They guard their environment as they would their family's safety.

Action Step #1

Listen for a negative conversation. How many days or hours did it take before you heard one? Take a proactive role and interfere ending the negativity.

Action Step #2

At the end of one day, go over the day and count how many uplifting conversations you had, how many neutral conversations you had, and how many conversations where someone was spoken of in a derogatory way. Be honest.

An Example

Professor Robert L. Humphrey, who died in 1997, was a civilian who worked with the military in both "cold" and "hot" wars in southern Italy, Turkey, Korea, Okinawa, Thailand, and Vietnam. His expertise was "Life Value." His job was to change the anti-US sentiments of the "Ugly American." General Charles Krulak said Humphrey's program saved the Marine Corps. Here is a story about Humphrey and negative talk. It's called "The Hunting Story."

After the war, America was the undisputed leader of the world. For a while everyone loved us, even our former enemies. But soon people began to resent us due to our superior attitudes and we Americans thought that was unjustified and ungrateful. In one particular country, the unrest was beginning to have strategic implications during that delicate time of detente. Dr. Humphrey's job was to solve that.

The basic problem was that the Americans working in that poor ally country thought that the local people were smelly, ignorant, violent, dishonest, and lazy, and let them know it. No matter what he did, Dr. Humphrey couldn't stop the negative talk, partially because some of it was true! As a result, though, the local people wanted the Americans to go home.

One day, as a diversion, Humphrey decided to go hunting for wild boar with some people from the American embassy. They took a truck from the motor pool and headed out to the boondocks, stopping at a village to hire some local men to act as guides.

This village was very poor. The huts were made of mud and there was no electricity or running water. The roads were unpaved dirt and the whole village smelled. Flies abounded. The men looked surly and wore dirty clothes. The women covered their faces and the children had runny noses and were dressed in rags.

It wasn't long before one American in the truck said, "This place stinks." Another said, "These people live just like animals." Finally, a young air force man said, "Yeah, they got nothin' to live for; they may as well be dead." What could you say? It seemed true enough.

But just then, an old sergeant in the truck spoke up. He was the quiet type who never said much. In fact, except for his uniform, he kind of reminded you of one of the tough men in the village. He looked at the young airman and said, "You think they got nothin' to live for, do you? Well, if you are so sure, why don't you just take my knife, jump down off the back of this truck, and go try to kill one of them?"

There was dead silence in the truck. Humphrey was amazed. It was the first time that anyone had said anything that had actually silenced the negative talk about these local people. The sergeant went on to say, "I don't know either why they value their lives so much. Maybe it's those snotty nosed kids or the women in the pantaloons. But whatever it is, they care about their lives and the lives of their loved ones, same as we Americans do. And if we don't stop talking bad about them, they will kick us out of this country!"

Humphrey asked him what we Americans, with all our wealth, could do to prove our belief in the peasants' equality despite their destitution? The sergeant answered easily, "You got to be able to look them in the face and let them know, just with your eyes, that you know they are men who hurt like we do, and hope like we do, and want for their kids just like we all do. It is that way or we lose."

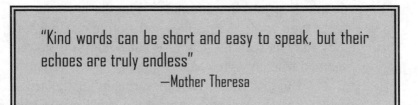

"Kind words can be short and easy to speak, but their echoes are truly endless"
—Mother Theresa

Break the Sound Barrier

—Leaders press forward faster when they are scared while average people slow down

One of my favorite stories I use in keynote talks is about Chuck Yeager breaking the sound barrier.

The government had planes and pilots capable of breaking the sound barrier prior to Yeager. The first pilot went up and the faster he went, the more the plane shook—violently. And the more the plane shook, the more frightened he became. Finally, the test pilot tried to slow the plane down and it crashed and he was killed.

A second pilot went up. The exact same thing occurred. The faster he went, the more the plane shook and the more the plane shook the more frightened he became. He, too, tried to slow the plane down and crashed and was killed.

Then Chuck Yeager went up. All the same things happened: the speed, the violent shaking, being afraid, etc.

It's OK to be frightened. We live in a scary world. If you are not somewhat frightened as a parent or business owner, you're living in a fantasyland.

As Chuck Yeager tells this story, he thought if he was going to die, he was going to die in style. So, instead of trying to slow down, he went faster.

Boom! He broke the sound barrier.

One message here is that as you go for your goal and you are getting scared and want to slow down, don't! SPEED UP! Take even more massive action.

Slowing down, you'll crash, and speeding up you break through to your goal and to a higher level of achievement.

Where in your life are you being tempted to slow down? How can you take even more massive action and break through?

Perhaps you are in network marketing and you are tempted to put off qualifying for a higher compensation level for another quarter. How can you take more action, immediately, rather than putting it off?

Whatever your situation, pick one area of your life this week and take massive action.

TAKEAWAY!

When you are out of your comfort zone going for a goal and are scared, go faster, not slower. Your capability is never the question. Your commitment is.

Action Step #1

Identify one goal you have been putting off because you have been afraid you couldn't do it or wouldn't have the money or time to do it. Now, make a commitment to move forward this week in spite of that fear.

Action Step #2

Identify one goal you have failed at achieving. What is a new way of thinking or approaching it that you haven't tried?

An Example

At one point in my professional life, I had been working 18 years for a company. I knew I should no longer stay there, because ethically, I was no longer in alignment with what they were doing.

At the same time I was scared to do anything else. I had a wife and three children and substantial monthly payments. My job was secure for life there at just under $100,000 a year.

I had seen other people who had been good trainers leave and fail. It was a classic case of my plane shaking and me wanting to slow down.

It was almost Christmas and I was thinking that maybe I should leave around the fourth of July, US Independence Day, as a symbolic act.

Then, with my family gathered together, we had a discussion and we decided to take massive action that very week! By New Year's Day, I was out on my own, without even a game plan, starting a new company. We made a profit our first month and have never looked back.

Wherever you are in life, NOW is a great time to take massive, bold action!

"Avoiding danger is no safer in the long run than outright exposure. The fearful are caught as often as the bold"

—Helen Keller

Solve Your Own Problems

—Leaders do not support those claiming to be a victim by solving their problems for them

In our seminars we have people explore the whole notion of "being victim," which is the viewpoint where something is done to you.

Anytime you see a family member or employee or down-line partner playing victim, you will usually see two other roles being played: Rescuer and Persecutor.

The rescuer solves the problem for the victim while the persecutor blames or attacks the victim. Imagine a wife goes a little victim by saying to her husband, "Gee, I just don't have anything to wear."

Now, the husband steps into the rescuer role by saying, "Well, why don't you just wear the blue outfit." He has now solved the problem for his wife, the victim.

But now, the wife will move into the persecutor role and say, "No, silly, I wore that one last week." So, the husband slides into the victim role, and goes, "You're always picking on me."

She now moves into the rescuer role by saying, "There, there, it's OK. I'll take care of you honey."

Now, he moves over into the persecutor role with this, "I don't need you to take care of me!"

On and on it goes. It is a vicious never-ending cycle. The same scenario goes on with parents, and children, and employees, and bosses or down-line and up-line. The only way to end it is by being a leader and operating from "responsible" and causing everyone else to operate from responsible, too.

Once you step into either one of these roles, you're caught.

Many times, we will try and solve someone else's problem thinking that we are being a giver (it also makes us feel good). Then we don't have time to solve our own challenges and we go victim to the people we supervise.

Maybe it is being more of a giver to hold them as capable and cause them to solve their own problems.

Make a list right now of a place where you have stepped into each role. Is there one role you adopt more than the other?

TAKEAWAY!

Leaders do not solve other people's problems. They support other people in solving their own problems.

Action Step #1

Identify one area where you have solved someone else's problem. Role-play with a friend or associate how you cannot solve their problem, yet still be compassionate.

Action Step #2

Find one area where you are in some small way persecuting someone for being a victim. How can you support the person in being solution oriented?

An Example

In my very first piece of rental property, I rented to someone who was struggling financially. I thought I was doing them a favor. (They were being victim and I was playing the rescuer).

Pretty soon, they could not pay the rent. I thought I would be a good guy and said basically, "Hey, pay me when you can." (More rescuer.)

At two months overdue I started to inquire what was going to happen as far as me getting paid. Lo and behold they started blaming ME for their problems.

Imagine my surprise! I was hurt and confused. I started telling all my friends how society had gone downhill and you just couldn't get good people as tenants anymore. (Now, I had shifted over to victim).

At the time, I was unaware of this game so there is no happy ending to the story. I was out several month's rent and my tenants left with a bad taste in their mouths.

Many times since, I have been in this same situation in business. It took me awhile to learn the lesson. I recently did a speaking engagement and the person had trouble paying me due to financial reversals in other areas of his life. I set a firm, renegotiated, written way for him repaying me. When he was about to miss the first payment, he tried to renegotiate again. I said, "No. This doesn't serve you. Find another way to solve the problem. I expect to be paid as agreed. I will brainstorm ways with you if you want, but I expect to be paid tomorrow."

This was hard for me. It still is. But it was the right thing to do for him and me.

The next day he handed me the money. He felt better and I did, too. Now, he doesn't avoid me out of guilt and he holds himself in higher esteem.

"Consider how hard it is to change oneself and you'll understand how impossible it is to change others"
—Jacob Braude

The Whole Truth and Nothing But

—Leaders are radically honest with themselves and others

I graduated from West Point, the United States Military academy. There was a simple rule there that if you ever lie, cheat, or steal even once, or tolerate someone who does then you are thrown out.

Having made it through four years without ever having lied, cheated, or stolen, I considered myself an honest man. Then, in my first seminar with my mentor, Tom, the group I was in was asked to go around and tell people what really exciting result each of us wanted to create out of the weekend seminar (equivalent to our Personal Mastery weekend today).

What I really wanted was a wildly romantic long-lasting relationship, but I noticed I was telling people that I wanted to be better organized. Since I really did want to be more organized, it wasn't technically lying, but it also was not the truth.

There are many ways we hide from the truth. Being rigorously honest with yourself and others is key to leadership. Many people will fudge the truth all the time, especially if it is uncomfortable or inconvenient. Many people compromise honesty when the business results they expect are not there. They fail to tell the truth, believing that the truth will hurt them, but then the wrong adjustments are made by management because of inaccurate information.

In politics, so few people tell the truth that the majority of people are cynical and don't even bother with the process. In a personal setting, we don't tell the truth to ourselves and we fail to make the necessary adjustments to get our life on track.

One way to fudge the truth is to simply not give honest feedback, whether to others or ourselves. There are people who never make an asset and liability statement up because they are afraid of the answer. They never go get a medical check-up because they are afraid of the answer. They never asked a spouse a difficult question because they don't want to grapple with the possible conflict it will unearth.

CEOs and managers seldom ask for input from employees or clients in order to avoid having to deal with the feedback. As a manager, you may ask someone on your team, "How many phone calls did you make?" The person may fudge the truth by being vague and say, "A lot." You then try and get more specific and ask, "How many calls is 'a lot'?" The person says, "25." Then you ask, "Were those all live calls or were some of those left messages?"

Leaders are not only honest themselves, but they train their people to be rigorously honest and to be proactive with the truth and to not be afraid of the truth. It is the only way proper course corrections can be made.

Like everything else, honesty has both benefits and prices. The prices to honesty should not be ignored. This does not mean you tell everything to everybody. Nor does it mean you relieve your guilt by sharing something from your past in a relationship that has no current relevance.

It does mean being honest in your assessment of the prices and benefits. How honest have you been on a scale of 1-10 in the last year? What is your commitment for this next week with the people at work, home, and the community?

TAKEAWAY!

Honesty is a matter of both being truthful in what you say AND in the full disclosure around a topic. Leaders create an environment where people feel safe enough to be honest and train their people to tell the truth.

Action Step #1

Spend 10 minutes making a list of what you have been pretending not to know in your personal and professional life.

Action Step #2

Ask your most significant personal and professional relationship what he or she has been afraid to tell you. Ask that person what consequence he or she was afraid would happen that they were trying to avoid.

An Example

I had an employee who had done a good job for us for a number of years, but due to changing circumstances in the person's life and in our company's needs, the individual was no longer performing up to standard.

For many months we on the management team would make comments, but no one had that honest, tough conversation with the individual. We did not want to admit that at some level we had failed the employee. It hurt our ego.

Everyone would give input to the individual on what to do differently, but everything was met with resistance. No one had the big discussion: "Is it time for you to move on?"

We conned ourselves in a dozen ways. We told ourselves we were good and could turn the person around. We said it was a temporary problem and the person needed space. On and on.

There is a technical, psychological term for this: Cognitive Dissonance. That's where our beliefs and behavior do not match up. The phenomenon is that people suppress certain aspects or facts of reality because if they told the truth to themselves it would hurt their self image.

When we finally sat with this individual and confronted the big question, we still deluded ourselves and gave the person another year to change. We did not want to face reality.

Another year later we had the discussion and the person moved on and was actually relieved. That person had also not wanted to tell the truth about the changes that had occurred and had covered up the truth with feelings of guilt for thinking of leaving. Once the final decision had been made, literally everyone, including this person, was much better off.

"As scarce as truth is, the supply has always been in excess of demand"
—Josh Billings

Welcoming Objections
—Leaders embrace and enjoy objections to their plans

As you already know, we are all in sales, which is nothing but the ability to communicate in a way that causes action. Getting our children to study or having employees get behind a project is sales.

In the course of selling, we often run into objections. People feel they don't have time or money, don't want to work hard and be paid less, etc. There are countless other objections.

How would you like never to fear the word "no" or any other objection ever again? Most people see objections as the enemy, which must be fought.

The problem with this mindset is that in fighting objections you are fighting the very people you are trying to lead. *Leaders re-frame objections into friends and actually welcome objections.*

Why? Because objections provide needed information. Objections can tell us what a person really wants and is looking for, which is essential in selling to them.

How's that for a different set of sunglasses! By knowing objections up front, you can prepare people so they will achieve their goal instead of failing by being unprepared.

Here is a simple formula for handling any objection: the Three Fs: FEEL, FELT, FOUND. The first F is, "I know how you FEEL." The second, "I've FELT the same way." The third F is, "Here's what I've FOUND."

Suppose someone tells you they don't have the money to afford an offer you have for them.

Step #1: "I know how you FEEL."

Now, perhaps you're thinking, "What if I haven't felt the same way?" You have. *Everyone has the same feelings, just not at the same time or around the same circumstances.*

Have you ever felt sad, neglected, lonely, not wanted, inadequate, apathetic, elated, angry, content, etc.? Simply think of a different circumstance where you have felt the same way, so you are coming from integrity.

Step #2: "I've FELT the same way." This identification with the other person puts you both going in the same direction, instead of fighting them and making them wrong.

Step #3: "What I FOUND was that if the value is high enough, we will find a way to afford it. Let's look at the value you expect to get from this." This step is where you turn the person in a new direction. It's MUCH easier to turn a person around when you are going in the same direction with them.

In our advanced leadership seminar, we use the martial art of aikido to demonstrate this. When an arm and fist is coming at you, you do not push back. You move to the side, grab the arm, and move your body in the flow of their energy to turn them away.

You also must protect the attacker as much as yourself. A most unusual and effective idea if you are about creating a world that works for everyone with no one left out.

Suppose a team member tells you he doesn't have time to get a project done. Your response could be, "I know how you feel. I've felt the same way. What I found is that whenever you want something done, you go to a busy person, because they understand time management. Let's look at where you might be able to make the time."

The idea behind the Three Fs is non-resistance. You don't make the person wrong for having the objection.

Excitedly await your first objection this week and start practicing.

TAKEAWAY!

Objections are your friends. They provide needed information. The Three F's—FEEL, FELT, FOUND—are a way to overcome any objection without resistance.

Action Step #1

Identify something you want done by someone that you are pretty sure will resist. Get a friend and have them role-play the objections while you role-play the Three Fs.

Pre-planning and rehearsing your, "What I have found" to known objections will give you more confidence in the situation.

Action Step #2

Recall a conversation that has already occurred where objections came up and the conversation ended "poorly." Again, rehearse with a friend how you could have done it differently using the Three Fs. Then, go back and reopen the conversation with that person using the Three Fs.

An Example

Recently, one of our employees wanted to buy a house in California where our corporate offices are located. The person did not have any money and the cost of housing here is very high.

I want all our employees to be wealthy, because they will be good stewards with their wealth and owning a home is part of learning that.

I used the Three Fs: "I know how you feel. I felt the same way back in 1980" and I related my situation. I said that what I found was that you can buy a home with no money, no credit cards, and not know any wealthy people. What I found was that the lessons I learned in doing that have served me many times over since then and were financially more valuable than the house I bought (which has made me over a million dollars since selling and buying up). I went through how I purchased a house with none of my own money and the mindset doing that required.

I did not make him wrong for his objections. We embraced them as a good thing that would teach him lessons he needed to know to make our Klemmer & Associates business even bigger.

He located an eleven-acre piece of property and we started brainstorming how to finance it and build a house. He proceeded to put $2500 down and got his offer accepted. He still did not have the financing worked out, although we had some ideas.

At this point, a church stepped in and purchased the property before he even closed escrow for $300,000 more than he was going to pay. So, at the closing, he netted $150,000 and the investor realtor (also a graduate of our seminars) who brought the church in also netted $150,000.

Our employee embraced the objection of not having money and consequently has risen above that circumstance. Most people resist the objection and will not think about it, much less talk about it with others.

"Success is to be measured not so much by the position one has reached in life as by the obstacles which he had to overcome"

—Booker T Washington

What Are You Committed To?

—Leaders are committed to results, not reasons

Most people are committed to reasons not results. They want to appear reasonable. People often invoke "Be reasonable" as a good thing. It's not necessarily so.

You can be reasonable and that makes sense to people, but you don't produce the desired result. *You usually get only one or the other: reasons or results.*

As with everything, there are benefits and prices for both commitments. You simply need to decide which set of benefits you want and which set of prices you are willing to pay.

A commitment to reason has the benefits of being reasonable, removes guilt and blame, and is more convenient and comfortable. The prices attached to a commitment to reason are no results, your word has no power, and your self-esteem goes down.

The benefits of a commitment to results start with just that—results regardless of circumstances. Wow! That's powerful!

The prices attached to a commitment to results are that you face rejection, its more uncomfortable, and can cost you time, money, and energy. You need to decide consciously and up-front, not by default.

Everyone is committed. Unfortunately, many people are not committed to what they think they are committed to. Reasons or results, you are committed to one or the other.

Vince Lombardi, the legendary football coach of the Green Bay Packers, used to gather his players together in the locker room before the game. He would tell them that in a few hours they would be back in that very locker room and they'd have one of two things: reasons or results. And he'd ask, "What is it going to be?"

I'm going to suggest it was no accident Lombardi turned a "one win eleven loss" team into super bowl players. He had consistent winners. He got his players clear that their commitment was to results.

At that point, it did not matter if it rained, was below freezing, or even if Fuzzy Thurston got a detached retina or Bart Star broke his arm. Those were just reasons the team would find their way around.

If you are committed to reasons, you will sound reasonable, but you will not produce results. What kind of a life do you want to live? What are you committed to?

TAKEAWAY!

Being reasonable is not necessarily a good thing. You make sense, but often do not do what could be done to solve the problem.

Action Step #1

Make a list of the reasons you have been committed to this week, instead of results. Now, write the statement, "I am committed to results and not reasons" on a piece of paper. Put it somewhere you will see it frequently.

Action Step #2

Make a commitment to a least one result this week and become unreasonable.

An Example

About 20 years ago, I had a new facilitator working with me. We both lived in California and were scheduled to do a workshop in Vancouver, Canada, between Christmas and new Years. He really would rather have stayed home with his family.

We arrived at the airport and discovered a snowstorm had closed the Vancouver airport. He said we had done all we could do and recommended we should return home.

I replied, "100 people have bought tickets for this event and we will speak tonight in Vancouver."

I told him, "Get on the phones and find any airport we can get into anywhere near Vancouver and we'll drive the rest of the way."

He found we could get into Portland, Oregon, but it would not allow us time to drive and make it to our event on time.

I said, "Book the flights." He complained it was useless, but I told him we would figure out the rest of the solution on the way. We were moving forward.

I then got on the phone and asked our sponsor in Vancouver to research charter planes and if we could land at a smaller airport nearby. By the time we arrived in Portland, she had located a charter flight that dropped cargo off in Vancouver and was going to return empty to a private field that was open. For a nominal fee, we became the return cargo.

We spoke in Vancouver that night on time! My new facilitator got a valuable lesson in what a commitment to results was and how very different that looked from a commitment to being reasonable.

> "In every battle there comes a time when both sides consider themselves beaten, then he who continues the attack wins."
> —Ulysses S. Grant

Doing Things Differently

—Leaders make use of psychological trigger devices

One of the simplest and yet most powerful tools for change that I've ever come across is called a psychological trigger device.

A psychological trigger device is a fancy term for anything that triggers you into a different way of thinking, feeling, or behaving. It gets you off being on automatic.

Did you ever have a song you associated with a particular person? Years later, even if you weren't in that relationship anymore, you hear that song and it triggers all kinds of feelings. That song was a trigger device.

In our Personal Mastery Seminars, we start every session with the same song.

It helps the participants be seated on time. After the seminar is over, if they hear that song, it triggers all the memories of the seminar even to the point of making them feel like they should get a chair and be seated!

We encourage our students to write concepts like the 3R's (Resentment-Resistance-Revenge) on a piece of paper and put it around a ketchup bottle in the refrigerator. Then, when they're doing a mundane activity—like opening the refrigerator—that triggers them to think about the concept.

Remembering to think about a concept when we are in our normal routine is the hardest part. I probably have 25 eagles of all types in my house. I have porcelain eagles, crystal eagles, and wooden eagles, even eagle cuff links.

Eagles have vision. They can spot a dime from one-quarter of a mile away. So, when I see an eagle it triggers me to think long term about my life and my company, versus what is happening this year.

You can have negative triggers in your life as well as positive triggers. I've seen people who have recently been divorced wear their wedding ring on a different finger. I recommend they think about what it is triggering their subconscious to think about. If it's reminding them they are a failure at relationships, then it is a negative trigger and they should get rid of it.

Your clothes will trigger feelings and thoughts. Look in your closet. What do you hear various pieces of clothing saying to you? Your car is a trigger, too. What does it tell you?

Leaders take control of their environment by putting positive triggers around them and removing any negative triggers.

TAKEAWAY!

Trigger devices are anything that triggers you to feel differently than you do in the moment. Use the triggers to help you get what you want.

Action Step #1

List three concepts you want to remind yourself of. Now, write out a statement or go buy something that represents those three concepts and put them all around your car and house.

Action Step #2

Walk around your house. Look in your closet and garage. Look at your car. Look around your desk at work.

Make an assessment of what things are positive and negative triggers. Remove the negative triggers wherever possible.

An Example

There was a time in my life when I recognized that I was avoiding the uncomfortable and more difficult things I knew I had to do. It made the day drag by as I dreaded doing certain things. I knew if I would just knock the hard tasks out first, my day would have more energy and creativity.

I took a regular sheet of paper and wrote in big, bold letters: GUOYAAGDI.

I taped it to the back of my front door so it was the last thing I saw before going to work. I would sometimes shout it like a cheer as I went out the door and got into my car.

It stood for, "Get Up Off Your Ass And Go Do It." It was a great trigger device to get me to tackle the tough things first.

Later, I had a brass plaque of GUOYAAGDI made for my desk and it sits there today.

"Daring ideas are like chessmen moving forward. They may be beaten, but they may start winning the game."
—Goethe

Anything Is Possible

—Leaders are always attempting the impossible

I have a sign in my house that reads, "He who attempts the impossible has little competition." Have you ever thought about that?

All the competition is down at the bottom. In the corporate world, all the competition is for the hourly paid jobs. There is no competition at the top.

It reminds me of the movie "Jonathan Livingston Seagull" and the opening scene with all the seagulls fighting for scraps of fish floating in the ocean. Then the camera pans up to the sky and Jonathan is soaring high above . . . alone.

What impossible thing are you willing to go after this week? If you are in sales, can you attempt to communicate with an impossible number of prospects? Are you willing to even let yourself think of how you would get to an impossible number of prospects?

Can you attempt to have what you view to be an impossibly fun week? Can you let yourself attempt to have an impossible romantic evening?

A wise business mentor once told me that he ripped the word "impossible" out of his dictionary. When one of his children said something was impossible, he would reply, "There is no such word." When the child would argue he'd hand them the dictionary and challenge them to find the word "impossible." It wasn't there.

To most people, possible is merely a reference made about what they have already seen others do. It's common knowledge that at one time breaking the four-minute mile was thought to be "impossible." The human body physically couldn't do it.

Once Roger Bannister broke the four-minute mile, half a dozen people did it shortly thereafter. Within several years, over 300 people had run four-minute miles and today they are doing it in high school.

Decide, right now, what impossible thing you are going to let yourself think about this week and actually attempt. For the moment, don't even worry about whether you achieve it. Simply experience putting yourself in the realm where there is no competition.

TAKEAWAY!
Impossible is usually a relative term based on past experiences you have seen.

Action Step #1

Write the saying, "He who attempts the impossible has little competition," on a piece of paper and tape it to the dash of your car. It will trigger you to risk at a level beyond your norm.

Action Step #2

Take something you want to do that you think is impossible, such as buy a house with no money. Sit with two people who are more successful than you and brainstorm the possibilities.

For example, not long ago I sat with someone in Toronto, Canada, who saw a $650,000 piece of property he wanted, but thought it was impossible for him to get it. I asked whether the down payment or the monthly cash flow was the problem?

He said he had saved money and could make the down payment, but he couldn't afford the monthly payment. I asked if he knew that there were people with the opposite problem who could afford the extra monthly, but did not have the down payment? He could see that.

I asked what would happen if he asked them to pay the $1,000 a month he was short and they received a part interest in the house? That way, they got involved in real estate appreciation without a down payment and he got into his house.

He hadn't thought of that. Then he said, "You know, there is a basement I could rent out for $500, too." Already the world of possibilities was opening up for him.

An Example

The mission of Klemmer & Associates is to develop the bold, ethical, compassionate leaders who will create a world that works for everyone with no one left out. To most people that is audacious.

No one left out means everyone is literate, everyone has enough to eat, everyone has clean water and shelter, and everyone has meaningful work.

Will that happen in my lifetime? I doubt it.

Is it an impossible dream that has brought into being some spectacular successes? Yes.

Already, we have just signed a deal for doing our work in Saudi Arabia. We also hope to do our work in the United States Congress and Senate, which would revolutionize how this country spends our money.

We are on our way, one step at a time.

"While they were saying among themselves it couldn't be done, it was done"

—Helen Keller

Commitment vs. Compliance

—Leaders generate true commitment in those around them, instead of compliance

Leaders generate true commitment in those around them, instead of compliance. A key principle for leaders— whether in sales, parenting, management, or community action—is distinguishing commitment vs. compliance.

Compliance is the mindset when people do something merely because they feel they have to. Many employees go to work out of compliance. Children often attend school or keep a curfew out of compliance. People will serve on school boards or be in a marriage out of compliance.

Think about one area you are in compliance. Don't brush this off. Everyone has an area like that. What is your experience of compliance? It's probably tiring, there is no passion, and you produce minimal results.

Commitment *is where you have totally surrendered to a choice you have made.* Name one area of your life or one thing where you have given up any thoughts other than doing it. You are totally committed.

What is your experience of commitment? It may require a lot of work, but it is fun, energizing, and you produce maximum results. You feel bulletproof.

If you are in a network marketing team selling and have trouble duplicating, it is because your people are compliant, not committed. If you are in any job and your department is not producing, it is because they are in compliance.

How do you generate commitment in people vs. compliance?

You find out what's in it for them. When people are clear about what's in it for them, they will be committed.

TAKEAWAY!

Move yourself and others into commitment from the compliance by finding out what's in it for them.

Action Step #1

Identify people in your life that you feel are in compliance with you. Have a conversation with them about what they are experiencing. Now, have an open conversation about what's in it for them should they produce the result you want.

Action Step #2

Find an area of your life that is flat—has no energy. Take a half-hour to dig down into what is really in it for you by doing it. Take another half-hour brainstorming with someone not attached to the outcome as to what could be in it for you.

An Example

Jay, the chairman of the board of one of our corporate clients, had taken both our Personal Mastery and Advanced Leadership seminars. He was about to start our executive coaching program.

To make the initial meeting with his fellow executives he was going to have to get up at 5 am. He noticed that he was not excited about getting up so early. He already saw himself as tired, and was silently grumbling about the earliness of the meeting.

He noticed the unpleasant experience he was creating for himself as a sign of compliance.

Jay then started to examine why he had decided to do the coaching program in the first place. He saw that what was in it for him was setting an example for his fellow executives by showing up totally committed. And he saw the other executives getting full value out of the program, as well as what would happen with creating a context in the corporation of commitment versus compliance.

He showed up at the early morning meeting with a great attitude and was so impressed with the results that he called our marketing director, Steve Hinton, and shared what had happened.

Compliance can happen to the best of us and we all can move ourselves to commitment. The event was the same for Jay, but the experience was vastly different.

"Until one is committed, there is hesitancy, the chance to draw back, always ineffectiveness. Concerning all acts of initiative (and creation), there is one elementary truth the ignorance of which kills countless ideas and splendid plans: that the moment one definitely commits oneself, the providence moves too. A whole stream of events issues from the decision, raising in one's favor all manner of unforeseen incidents, meetings and material assistance, which no man could have dreamt would have come his way.'
—William Murray

Extraordinary challenges
—Leaders take on extraordinary challenges

Admiral Halsey was a graduate of the Naval Academy and a famous admiral in World War II. During the war, he was commanded to stall the Japanese navy for 24 hours.

The problem was that he only had small ships and he would be up against battleships, aircraft carriers, and destroyers. If he couldn't stop them for 24 hours, there would be major negative consequences to the United States in terms of loss of lives, equipment, and position.

He ended up stalling the Japanese navy for almost 36 hours and it was a turning point for the United States in the Pacific. In that battle, however, more senior naval officers were lost than in all of the rest of World War II combined! In essence, he had sent many of his academy classmates to their deaths. He was crying afterwards and an aide tried to console him by saying, "Sir, they were all great men."

Admiral Halsey replied with what I feel is a classic line in history. He said, *"There are no great men. There are only ordinary men who take on great challenges."*

Think about the great achievements and many times there were plenty of talented people who could have done something, but usually it is accomplished by someone who simply had the courage and vision to go for it. It is not so much talent, as the willingness to take on extraordinary challenges that separates the average from the super successful.

TAKEAWAY!

The willingness to take on an extraordinary challenge brings out the extraordinary in ordinary people. Don't wait for others. You make the extraordinary happen!

Action Step #1

What level of challenges have you been willing to take on? This week, think about what extraordinary challenge you are willing to take on.

Action Step #2

Interview someone you have contact with who, from your viewpoint, has accomplished something extraordinary. Ask where they felt inadequately equipped or prepared.

An Example:

My mentor, Tom, was a man of ordinary beginnings. He did not go to college. Actually, he went one semester and got thrown out. He stuttered until his twenties. He was not born into money.

In 1973 when his mentored died, he started his own company. Even at that time he had very little money. Two years later his mentor's ranch became available for sale at a government auction. It was 2,000 acres and the asking price was $3,500,000!

His company at the time was grossing less money than the monthly payment would be on the ranch, but Tom felt he should have the ranch. He assembled a team to rise to the occasion. He spent two days forming and melding the team into a mastermind. They were mobilized by an extraordinary opportunity and became extraordinary.

They purchased that ranch and it became the centerpiece of his company. Tom affected thousands of people in a very significant way during his lifetime. He was an ordinary man who rose to extraordinary challenges time after time.

"Courage is the price life extracts for granting peace"
—Amelia Earhart

Where Is Your Replacement?

—Leaders train and replace themselves with others who are better than themselves

Average people are so insecure and afraid they will not have a job that they do not hire competent people beneath them and then do not train them in all the things they know. But leaders are so confident and think multi-generationally that they hire people better than themselves and then spend a significant amount of time training them.

In the days of sailing ships and kings and queens, there was a wise king who had three sons. Instead of the tradition of appointing the oldest as king, he wanted to pick the wisest son as king. He decided to test each one.

He took the oldest on a hunting trip. In the middle of the afternoon he said, "Take an arrow, point it at yonder tree, and tell me what you see."

As the oldest son was pointing the arrow he realized he was being tested and decided to impress his father. He said, "Father, I see a bird sitting on a limb. What's more, I see where the limb is connected to the tree. I see beyond this tree to a whole forest of trees. I see where these trees will be cut down and be used to build ships. I see where the ships will travel around the world."

He went on and on. Meanwhile the bird flew off. The king said he was certainly impressed with all the son could see.

The next day the king took the second son out on a hunting trip. At the point of the test, the second son realized he too was being tested and also decided to impress the king. As he pointed his arrow he said, "Father, I see a bird on a limb. I see where the limb is connected to the trunk of the tree. I see where the trunk points to the stars in the sky. I see beyond this sky to the galaxy. I see galaxies beyond the galaxies."

Meanwhile the bird flew off. The king said he was certainly impressed.

The next day he took the youngest son, who could barely pull a bow back. The test was the same. The youngest son said, "Father, I see where the bird's wing is connected to it's breast."

He let the arrow fly . . . and that night they ate.

The third son became king because he accomplished the king's goal: they were on a hunting trip and wanted food. Job done! And on top of it, the training of a replacement was not a threat to the king. He was working toward it.

Are you training your replacement or have you allowed yourself to get lost in grandiose schemes or the small details of paperwork? Does the idea of a replacement threaten you?

The king was training his replacement long before he needed to be replaced, but average people are threatened by training others and therefore never do. Leaders are confident they will always have more to offer the organization and begin the replacement process today.

TAKEAWAY!

Leaders actively look to be replaced . . . and actively train others to do just that. It is part of their job description.

Action Step #1

List the top five problems in your business or career. Pick one as the top problem. What action can you take today to educate someone in solving that pressing problem?

Action Step #2

Who are you training to replace yourself? How much of your time is spent training them? Discipleship is one of the four jobs of a leader. Make a list of people you can train to do what you do.

An Example:

Training replacements in an organization from your own family is especially difficult. One of the best transitions has been seen in the Marriott Corporation. The founder, Jay Williard Marriott, built it up from the ground floor, then started training several people as his replacement. One of those people was his son.

He did not play favorites. His son earned his own reputation by solving problems in the company. Along the way, Jay spent time coaching his son and his son worked hard to prove himself capable of leading the company. In the end, he did just that. The Marriott Corporation is booming today under his leadership.

> "Back 12 years ago, when Dr. Mathews was president here, we had a plan that when I got ready to quit, we'd bring a certain guy in and he'd take over that day and I'd leave. But as time wore on, I realized that wouldn't have been good at all."
>
> —Bear Bryant

The Speed of Recovery
—Leaders have a short recovery quotient

How long does it take you to bounce back from something? That is your recovery quotient.

Consider the salesperson who gets a single "no" and won't even try to sell for the rest of the day! Or the person looking for a date who gets rejected and won't ask anyone else out for a date for a month! Or someone who fails on a project and won't assume responsibility for another project for a year!

Everyone has failures, but the recovery quotient should not be that long. The truth is, successful people have more failures and rejection than average people. The real difference is in how quickly they bounce back.

There is a story of a donkey that fell into a deep well. Someone above was shoveling dirt filling in the well. Every time more dirt was thrown in the well, the donkey shook itself like a dog, thereby shaking off the dirt, and took a step forward . . . and eventually walked out of the hole.

Do you feel like dirt is being thrown on you? Can you shake it off and take a small step forward?

Five keys to quickly bouncing back are:
1) **look at someone who has it far worse than you**
2) **make it an ego battle** (Is this circumstance stronger or are you?)
3) **talk with people who overcame defeat** (ask what they did to bounce back)

4) **bring God into the matter** (this is a wise long-term spiritual approach)
5) **carry it out to the extreme** (can you handle a worst case scenario?)

TAKEAWAY!
Everyone gets knocked down, but champions bounce right back! Shake it off and get back in the fight!

Action Step #1

Think of your last setback that you have not moved forward from. Now go visit someone who has it far worse than you. Then begin to address your setback.

Action Step #2

Give yourself hope by interviewing someone who has suffered a defeat or setback and not only survived but thrived.

An Example:

In 1998, I had a woman sue me. It was in my viewpoint fraudulent. Through a series of events that seemed like a Greek tragedy, we unfairly lost $400,000!

I learned a lot about the difference between law and justice. I got schooled about the real world of business and how to protect yourself from unsavory characters.

It was one of those moments where you can either build your character or become bitter and settle for a mediocre life. We (my family and corporate family) worked on our recovery quotient. There were dark days of doubt, but we kept moving forward. I visited an aids clinic and a homeless shelter to get a better perspective on my own situation.

My wife and I looked the worst-case scenario (that of losing our house) squarely in the eye and said, "We could live with that." We prayed a lot and asked for the wisdom to see all the lessons we should learn and asked for God's guiding hand. I talked to people who had gone bankrupt, suffered the death of a spouse, and other setbacks who had bounced back.

In two short years, we were able to recover everything we had lost and more! I say this not to brag, because this pales in comparison to what others have bounced back from, but it is merely a very personal story to give you hope. Dark days may come, but there is light at the end of the tunnel!

"Our greatest glory is not in never falling, but in rising every time we fall."
—Confucius

Giving and Receiving Feedback

—Leaders are experts in giving and receiving feedback

How would you rate yourself on receiving feedback? How would you rate yourself on giving feedback?

Many people have difficulty in one or both. Companies pay our firm K&A Leadership Seminars Inc. large sums of money to have their people comfortable with giving and receiving feedback. Why? Because feedback is the breakfast of champions.

Without feedback, you are like a pilot flying a plane with no instruments. You can do it, but it is more difficult and you cannot fly in as many difficult conditions. The more feedback you have, the more information you have to make the corrections that will keep you on track.

Key #1 to receiving feedback is to realize feedback is not the truth. Many people are resistant to receiving feedback because they are concerned with what is true.

Imagine my children give me feedback that they don't feel loved by me. That certainly does not mean I don't love them, but since I am interested in a better relationship with them, then I want that feedback in order to know what I need to do differently so that they do feel loved.

Key #2 to receiving feedback is to learn to be "flat" around feedback. Don't get riled up. Just listen. Sometimes the feedback says more about the giver of the feedback than about you. Suppose the altimeter reading in a plane says you are at 20,000 feet. The instrument might be broke.

Key #3 to receiving feedback is to have multiple sources for feedback. A pattern in feedback is more valuable than one person's input because multiple feedback covers up individual agendas.

Feedback goes both ways. Leaders are also good at giving feedback.

Key #1 of giving feedback is to focus on making a contribution, not worrying about how others perceive you. Many are hesitant to give feedback because they are concerned that other people won't like them, will take revenge, or will not be supportive. They sacrifice results in order to be liked.

Key #2 of giving feedback is to think of feedback as merely offering one viewpoint of many and that with many viewpoints the other person will have a more complete picture. The idea that feedback must come from an "expert" is ridiculous.

Key #3 to giving feedback is to be unattached to its reception. You are not aiming to convince a person. You are merely offering your viewpoint. A great way to do this is to say, "My experience of . . ." and then explain your viewpoint. This makes it clear you are not stating what is true but are offering an experience or viewpoint.

Another way to help your feedback be received is to come from the perspective of A) What worked? B) What didn't work? C) What's next? This eliminates judgment and maintains a forward moving context.

TAKEAWAY!

Feedback is not the truth. It is a viewpoint. Without feedback it is hard to make the proper course corrections.

Action Step #1

Pair up with someone this week and practice giving and receiving feedback. Pick a simple topic, like how they might be dressed or why a certain type of car is preferred.

Action Step #2

Tell several people that you are practicing receiving feedback and would like them to give you feedback on a subject. Remember to be "flat" on receiving the feedback as they have not been trained on how to give it properly.

An Example:

When I first started doing presentations, I had no experience in public speaking. I practiced in front of trained presenters and then got critiqued on what worked and what didn't work. My only permitted response was, "Thank you" or "What did you mean?"

I copied their input in a journal, then started doing small group presentations. I was instructed to always bring someone along who would critique me. I added those notes to the journal.

In addition, I tracked the details related to the presentation, such as how many people attended, how much money we made, etc.

The results were great feedback. *In fact, results are the fairest way to gauge anything; often harsh, always fair.* If I thought I did great but no one enrolled, then I did things that didn't work or did not do things that could have worked. Over time, I became a full-fledged presenter in my mentor's seminars.

The feedback never stopped. We were instructed to constantly give feedback, even to my mentor! Feedback simply became a way of life.

"Advice is like castor oil, easy to give but dreadful uneasy to take"

—Josh Billings

Do You Trust Others?

—Leaders have a great capacity to trust

What is trust? Most people can see the benefit of trust in business (faster growth, teamwork, and open communication), but they have difficulty actually doing it! That is because trust requires that they trust other people, trust themselves, and trust that quiet small voice inside that knows in realms other than sight and sound.

This last type of trust is often called intuition and can be hugely effective in business because it allows you to make decisions with insufficient data. *Most decisions are in fact made with insufficient data.*

One way to better understand your intuition and to make better decisions is to clarify your "baseline response." A baseline is a benchmark or reference point. There are benchmarks on a sports field that tell you when you are in and where you are out of bounds. Your body has benchmarks that can tell you many things your intuition is trying to tell you but you cannot hear.

The "baseline response" technique is a way to use your body to know whether something is true or false, especially when your mind is confused by too much or not enough data.

To practice this, get with someone you feel comfortable with. Sit in a chair, relax, and close your eyes so you can concentrate. Have the other person say obviously false statements, like: 2 x 2 = 146, your hair is purple, you live on the moon, etc. Your job is to become aware of how your body responds with every false statement. You may notice your stomach tightens up or your hands get cold or hot or your muscles above your eyebrows tighten.

Whatever your response, that is your "baseline response" for falseness. If you are having a conversation with someone and that same physical reaction occurs, then go on full alert because something is not right. I often use it when hiring people, especially in areas like accounting that are not my expertise. (Take the time this week to find your baseline response and than begin looking for when it occurs.)

Does trust mean you just tell people to do something and forget about it? No! There are boundaries to your trust. Many employees and managers mistakenly think their boss doesn't trust them when the boss checks up on them.

If you have been scuba diving, you know that a diving buddy is there to check your air tank and help keep you safe. It is not that you are incompetent. Quite the contrary!

In business and life, it's the same thing. Competent people overlook things, so having a back up system in place helps you trust yourself and others even more. Circus people put nets up while they are learning so they can build their trust in their skill level.

Trust is a muscle that must be built on experience. Pilots are always checking the instruments, yet they trust the plane will fly. It is natural for things to get off course. By checking the instruments frequently and course correcting, there is never the need for major course corrections.

TAKEAWAY!

Inspect what you expect. Trust does not mean you do not check on anther person's actions. Trust means allowing someone the space to fail and calculate how much you can afford to lose if they do fail. Establish limits of your trust.

Action Step #1

What is something you currently do in your job that you can train someone else to do? Now find and train that person. Trust your ability to train and trust that person's ability to handle the job. Inspect what you expect, and then expect it!

Action Step #2

What decision have you been avoiding because you didn't trust yourself. What safety net can you put in place to enable you to trust yourself with the decision in case it doesn't work out?_

An Example:

At one point in my career with my mentor, I was hiring accountants and lawyers, even though I am not an accountant or lawyer. I used the "baseline response" every step of the way. I was looking for someone with international experience in accounting.

A woman came in for an interview. All she had ever done was keep her husband's small business books in our local town. Her resume did not appear to fit what we wanted. I told her to tell me about her strengths and weaknesses, and then as she started to talk I tuned her out. I listened to my body as I asked myself is this the right person for this job. My fingers started to tingle, which is my signal for truth. I then asked myself if I should go by the resume and my stomach tightened, which is my signal for falseness.

With those responses in hand, I hired her. She stayed with the company for a decade and was the glue that kept the company together during some very difficult financial times. She was, in fact, the perfect person for the job.

"The only way to make a person trustworthy is to trust them"
—H Stimson

The Inside Is What Counts

—leaders use pressure to reveal the best of the real you

Many years ago in a town in Thailand, a large plaster Buddha was discovered. It sat in a makeshift covering for 20 years before a temple was built to house it. When they tried to move it with heavy equipment, the plaster cracked.

They stopped and examined the damage they had caused. To their amazement, inside was a pure gold Buddha, standing 13 feet tall and weighing 5 tons!

The gold Buddha was apparently plastered and painted so that warring tribes threatening to take over the village would not steal it. For hundreds of years, no one knew there was a gold Buddha hiding inside the plaster.

In many ways, this is the story of our life. I believe the inside of everyone is more precious than a gold statue. Over our lifetime we cover it up with lies we buy about ourselves. We believe we aren't worthy or good enough for something. We believe we aren't capable of doing something. We believe we can't handle the pressure of a bigger job.

Sometimes we get so covered up with our beliefs that we can't even remember what is inside. Then we put pretty paint on the outside by attaining a degree or dressing fancy or acquiring a big house. We are afraid to look inside because we know its plaster.

Sometimes it takes pressure, like the heavy moving equipment, for the plaster to be cracked and the greatness to be discovered.

Take 15 minutes and make a list of great qualities you have displayed in the past but have let dim. Perhaps at one time you were supremely confident and now there is an area of self-doubt. Perhaps you displayed total trust in a person or concept and now are mistrustful. Or perhaps you simply had a passion or excitement for life and it has ebbed.

Now decide how you will put yourself under pressure so that something cracks and the gold has a chance to be displayed again. Many people think pressure is something to be avoided, but leaders create pressure. They proactively put in place a creative tension.

TAKEAWAY!

Our goodness is often covered up by our not-so-good beliefs, which is then painted over. Pressure is a good thing. It reveals what is inside.

Action Step #1

Write down an area where you were most recently challenged (i.e. marriage, finances, health, etc.). What did the challenge reveal? If you don't like what it revealed, you are still in the plaster. What gold remains hidden?

Action Step #2

Who do you know who has not discovered the beauty inside of them? What can you do to assist them in seeing that beauty? Can you offer them an opportunity? Can you offer them encouragement to persist past the plaster?

An Example:

In 1995, after spending almost twenty years helping build my mentor's company, I left. With new leadership, many things changed about the company. The split was not an amicable one. I was asked not to talk to any of the facilitators whom I managed for fear that I would take many of them with me. I left alone.

I decided to do business seminars instead of public seminars so as not to compete with them. At age 45 I was starting from scratch, with no clients, no business plan, and about $7,000/month in expenses. I was scared and excited at the same time. The pressure of all that brought out things in me I could not see on my own.

I would not have picked me as a business owner. I would not have picked me to write a best-selling book, with many more to follow. It deepened my faith in God. It strengthened my marriage and the intimacy with my children. It freed my creativity. It added new people to my life almost instantly.

In sum, it was one of the best business moves I have ever made. And yet, while it was happening, I felt tremendous pressure. It felt unfair, but it forced me to reveal who I really was rather than the pretty façade I was putting on.

"Everything that can be counted does not necessarily count; everything that counts cannot necessarily be counted"

—Albert Einstein

Size of the Problem = Size of the Leader
—The size of leaders is gauged by the size of the problem they can handle

Develop a culture where those around you solve the problems in front of them, where everyone wants to solve a problem to show how valuable they are.

This is vastly different than the average organization where people avoid problems by taking the it's-not-my-problem approach. They blame, they pass the buck, and they do anything and everything to avoid it.

That is typical, but you want to be part of an organization that fights over who gets to solve the problem! *All people have problems. Not being aware they have problems is perhaps the biggest problem.*

The difference between the successful and the average is that the successful people attack their problems— and solve them—one at a time. Average people address the same problems every month, over and over, without fixing anything.

Why do successful people go looking for problems to solve? Because problems create value! If you want to make a lot of money, then solve problems that others can't or won't. If you are in real estate and the only houses you can sell are those that everyone else can sell, and you can only sell them to the average buyer, then you will make the same amount of money as everyone else. When you can solve problems like how to sell to clients no one else wants to deal with or how to solve a finance problem others can't, then you make an inordinate amount of money.

TAKEAWAY!
Problems are a good thing. Problems create value. They are the path to what you want. Average people have the same problem everyday. It never changes or goes away. Solve it now.

Action Step #1

Ask your boss to tell you what the biggest problem is. Then explain that you want to try and solve it.

Action Step #2

Write down the ways you are avoiding a certain problem. Now, write down a way of embracing the problem beside every way you avoid it. Then get going!

An Example:

A gentleman named Tom is in a network marketing company. He is a very successful distributor with a large down-line and a solid 6-figure income. He developed a piece of software that would assist in tracking a team's performance, recruit people automatically, adapt to the usage of products creating a personal profile, and many other things.

It proved to be incredibly effective, but it affected the incomes of others in negative ways. Without going into the politics or details of the situation, he was threatened with losing his distributorship if he continued to use the system.

This was a serious problem, not only for the loss of income, but because he had spent tens of thousands of dollars developing this software.

Instead of ignoring the problem, he decided to adapt the software for other companies in both his industry and outside his industry. This was not something he ever consciously conceived of doing while developing the product. Initially, it was simply a product to make his job easier. Instead of collapsing in the face of the problem of losing his distributorship or wasting years and money in developing, he rose to the occasion and now has both his lucrative down line and a multi-million dollar software company that is about to go public.

He is a leader who can handle multi-million dollar problems.

> "Our team is well balanced-we have problems everywhere"
> —Tommy Prothro

Conclusion

Congratulations on having the discipline to finish all 52 lessons. It ranks you among the elite. The biggest lessons probably came not from having the information in your head, but the experiences you had in application. Whether it even worked or not is less important than the lessons you gleaned and take with you. If you have not already taken advantage of a Klemmer & Associates live seminar check out our website at Klemmer.com and pick a date to attend the weekend Personal Mastery. It's an investment that will change your life. GUARANTEED. And while you are at it, bring a friend and change their life. It's a gift that lasts a lifetime. We love to hear success stories so do not hesitate to share your success with us at mastery@klemmer.com

Here are some recommended resources on leadership:

Bob Harrison, President
Harrison International Ministry
Web Site: www.increase.org
Phone: 800-632-4653

John Maxwell
Web Site: www.The PackerGroup.com
Phone: 877-859-4073

Miles Monroe
Web Site: www.bfmmm.com
Phone: 242-461-6400

To reach Brian Klemmer or Klemmer & Associates:

BY PHONE:
(707) 559-7722

TOLL FREE:
(800) 577-5447

BY FAX:
(707) 762-1685

BY U.S. MAIL:
1340 Commerce St, Suite G
Petaluma, CA 94954

By E-mail:
mastery@klemmer.com

Champions Workshop

The Champions Workshop is a 2-½ hour fun, impacting, and experiential workshop based on the "Formula of Champions." Brian Klemmer has interviewed Olympic world record holding athletes, CEOs of major corporations, and successful people of all walks of life in an effort to find the common denominators and keys to success. *The Formula of Champions is the result!*

Have you ever wanted something but were stuck because you didn't know what to do? *Never again! Here is a formula for producing results when you have no idea what to do. You can put this to use immediately.*

Is there a gap between what you want and what you actually get? *Learn why what you want has nothing to do with what you create.*

Mail in the attached perforated postcard and you can attend for FREE! This power-packed, riveting workshop is one of many workshops offered by Klemmer & Associates worldwide. Regularly $59.00!

If you need further information, call 800-577-5447 or visit <u>www.klemmer.com</u>.